DANCE
Mind & Body

Sandra Cerny Minton, PhD

HUMAN KINETICS

Library of Congress Cataloging-in-Publication Data

Minton, Sandra Cerny, 1943-
    Dance, mind & body / Sandra Cerny Minton.
        p. cm.
Includes bibliographical references (p. 173) and index.
    ISBN 0-7360-3789-6 (soft cover)
    1. Dance--Psychological aspects. 2. Mind and body.   I. Title: Dance,
mind, and body. II. Title.
    GV1588.5 .M56 2003
    792.8'01'9--dc21

2002013206

ISBN: 0-7360-3789-6

Acquisitions Editor: Judy Patterson Wright; **Managing Editor:** Wendy McLaughlin; **Assistant Editor:** Kim Thoren; **Copyeditor:** Jan Feeney; **Proofreader:** Kathy Bennett; **Indexer:** Betty Frizzell; **Permission Manager:** Toni Harte; **Graphic Designer:** Robert Reuther; **Graphic Artist:** Tara Welsch; **Art and Photo Manager:** Dan Wendt; **Cover Designer:** Jack W. Davis; **Photographer (cover):** Joe Clithero of B & J Creative Photography; **Photographer (interior):** Joe Clithero, unless otherwise noted; **Illustrator:** Dick Flood; **Printer:** Bang Printing

Human Kinetics books are available at special discounts for bulk purchase. Special editions or book excerpts can also be created to specification. For details, contact the Special Sales Manager at Human Kinetics.

Printed in the United States of America   10   9   8   7   6   5   4   3   2   1

Human Kinetics
Web site: www.HumanKinetics.com

United States: Human Kinetics
P.O. Box 5076
Champaign, IL 61825-5076
800-747-4457
e-mail: humank@hkusa.com

Canada: Human Kinetics
475 Devonshire Road Unit 100
Windsor, ON N8Y 2L5
800-465-7301 (in Canada only)
e-mail: orders@hkcanada.com

Europe: Human Kinetics
107 Bradford Road
Stanningley
Leeds LS28 6AT, United Kingdom
+44 (0) 113 255 5665
e-mail: hk@hkeurope.com

Australia: Human Kinetics
57A Price Avenue
Lower Mitcham, South Australia 5062
08 8277 1555
e-mail: liahka@senet.com.au

New Zealand: Human Kinetics
P.O. Box 105-231, Auckland Central
09-523-3462
e-mail: hkp@ihug.co.nz

DANCE
Mind & Body

This book is dedicated to all my teachers through the years and to my husband, Clarence Colburn, whose patience and support helped me complete this work.

Contents

Acknowledgments

I would like to thank Darlene Handler for reading the first draft of this book, and Judy Patterson Wright for her insightful suggestions throughout the planning and revision phases. I would also like to extend my appreciation to those who posed for the photos: Laurence A. Curry, Jacob J. Mora, Jane Sokolik, and Tamara Rae Wilkins.

Introduction

As I watched a student practice a movement sequence in class, I began to wonder what this student had in mind as she danced, so I asked her. She answered that she had been thinking about her feet—a response that did not surprise me, because I noticed that she was using her feet in a very precise way. This student seemed to be less aware of the other parts of her body, however. In another class, I remember asking the students to describe how a movement combination felt in their bodies. The response of the second group was very telling—they had little to say. In fact, most of the students seemed surprised that I had even asked such a question. These experiences and others like them made me think about how the mind and body work together during the act of dancing and how this connection can be used to improve students' dance-making abilities.

The goal of this book is to help you connect your mind and body in a way that encourages you to take a fresh look at movement. By understanding movement principles such as alignment, observing body line and shape, and studying the messages you send with your movements, you will learn to look at movement as a way to use your mind to tune in to your body.

You can incorporate this mind-body connection through exploration (relatively short movement sequences based on cues from outside your body) and improvisation (longer movement sequences initiated by your own feelings, imagination, and experiences). With each experience you will be asked to reflect on what you were thinking and how each movement made you feel. These methods not only teach you the techniques to express yourself but also give you the creative insight to explore and create dances based on your own style. You are going to begin the creative movement experiences with exploration so you are ready for the greater freedom found in improvisation.

The first four chapters of this book include some basic information about your body and movement. In chapters 1 and 2 you will explore where your body moves and what your body does while moving. In chapters 3 and 4 you will explore how your body moves and with what or whom you move. In chapter 5 you will build on the previous explorations and improvisations to explore and understand basic movement principles such as alignment, centering, gravity, balance, breathing, and tension and relaxation.

Chapters 6 through 9 emphasize working in a creative way with the components of dance making. The visual aspects of dance movement such as lines, planes, group shapes, pathways, transitions, movement order, and patterns will be discussed. You will look at the messages you can send with your body through gestures, and you'll explore various symbols used in dance—both literal and abstract.

Chapter 8 explores the use of external sources of inspiration such as the visual arts, music, literature, drama, and architecture. Finally, chapter 9 helps you bring it all together by exploring the idea of a dance as a whole. Throughout this book, you will observe movement from both an external viewpoint (watching others move and watching yourself in a mirror) and an internal viewpoint (through your kinesthetic sense). You will also learn to create the basic building block of a dance— the movement phrase—and to link phrases together and vary them. For quick reference, a glossary of terms is provided at the end of this book.

My hope in writing this book is to encourage you to look at and explore movement in many ways. Learning to observe more fully and explore with confidence should help you develop greater body awareness and the ability to use your body as a tool in the creative process of dance making.

chapter

1

Creating Spatial Awareness

To become more conscious of yourself and your environment, you must observe the space around you and the way you move within that space. For example, how you move in a crowded room is different than how you move on an open stage. You may not realize it, but space is all around you—above, below, in front, behind, and at your sides. In a sense, space surrounds your body as a cocoon or envelope.

Think about the different ways you can move in the space around you. There are two basic ways you can move in space: You can stay in one spot and move (that is, by using *personal space*), and you can move by traveling through space (using *general space*). Moving within either type of space becomes much more complex, however, when you think about what part of your body moves and how you do the movements. For example, you can stay in one spot and dance by moving one part of your body, or you can stay in one spot and dance by moving your whole body.

You can describe the *where* of moving your body in space by looking at the direction in which you move, the level at which you move, and the pathway of your movements. If you reach your arm forward and then to the back, you are moving one part of your body in two different directions. Did you know that you can also do the same actions at different levels? Thus, you can reach forward or back while your arm is above your head, at waist level, or at a point even with your knees. You can also do the same two actions—reaching front and back—by using different pathways using a straight or curved path.

Personal Versus General Space

You are going to learn more about the where of moving in space by examining your actions as they occur in personal and general space. When you dance in personal space, you perform in the space immediately surrounding your body while you stay in one place. Sometimes such actions are called *nonlocomotor*, or *axial*, movements because you move parts of your body from or around your center. Actions such as reaching, stretching, bending, and twisting are nonlocomotor movements. When you dance through space, however, your movement takes place in general space. Let's look at examples of each use of space. If you stand in one spot with your feet planted on the floor and reach your arms in front of your body, you are moving in personal space (see figure 1.1). On the other hand, when you walk across space so that your whole body travels from one point to another, you are moving in general space.

The following two exercises are your chance to explore personal and general space so that you can learn how these movements feel in your body. In each case, you will be asked to move in response to a written description. In addition, it is also a good idea to come up with a mental picture based on the written description so that you know how your movements should look. Finally, you will be asked to check your movements to make sure they match the mental picture.

FIGURE 1.1   Reaching in personal space.

Identifying Personal Space

Begin by standing with your feet apart so that they are under your shoulders to give you a solid base. Now, move both arms, reaching them into the space around your body. As you do this, imagine that a bubble surrounds your body. Hold the picture of the bubble in your mind, and stretch your arms as far from the center of your body as possible. Try to touch all parts of the inside of the bubble. This means that you must move your arms above, below, forward, backward, and sideways so that your actions define the inside of the whole bubble. Then, repeat your movements while you are standing in front of a mirror to check whether you are touching all the surfaces of the inside of the bubble around your body. If this appears to be true, the movements you have just performed define the outer limits of your personal space. In this same exploration, your arms are what you are moving, while touching the inside of the bubble is where you are moving.

Identifying General Space

To understand general space, begin at one point in the room and walk throughout the available space. As you do this, you should find that the available space is limited by the size of the room and also by obstacles in the room. Now, continue to walk and imagine that your walking energizes the whole room. Try to travel throughout every inch of space, and remember where you have walked in the room to make sure that you have covered the whole space. After you complete this exploration, review your movements to see whether you have covered the entire space with your walking. You should have found that moving in general space gave you a lot more freedom than moving in personal space because you were able to travel throughout the available space. Moving in personal space, on the other hand, meant that you could only do movements that extended into the space immediately around your body.

Directions in Space

There are eight basic *directions* in which you can move your whole body or its parts. The directions front and back are the easiest to see, but it is also possible to move from side to side and in four diagonal directions. A simple way to visualize movements that travel front, back, and side to side is to think about tracing the shape of a cross with your movements. Actions on the four diagonals then trace an X. Of course, the center of both the cross and the X would fall at the center of your body or at the center of the room (see figure 1.2).

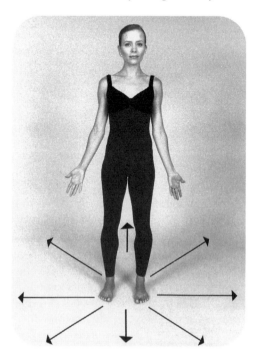

FIGURE 1.2   Eight basic directions of movement.

Identifying Directions in Personal Space

Review the eight basic directions and have a clear picture of all eight in your mind. Then, reach one arm out from your center into each of the eight directions. Remember to reach your arm out as far as possible so that you are stretching to the limits of your personal space. Repeat the same exploration using your other arm or one leg. If you decide to use your leg, you might want to place one hand on the wall or on another stable object to help you balance. Repeat this exploration in front of a mirror so that you can see whether you are moving a part of your body in eight different directions that describe a cross and an X that intersect at your center.

Identifying Directions in General Space

In this exploration, your actions will follow the eight directions, but this time you will be moving in general space. Begin by standing in the middle of the room with your body parallel to and facing one wall. Picture the eight directions in your mind. Walk forward in one direction, then return to the middle of the room. Repeat this process with each of the other seven directions so that when you are finished you have traced the shape of a cross and an X on the floor. Remember that the center of the cross and X intersect at the center of the room. Finally, do this same exploration in front of a mirror. Does it look as if you are traveling in eight different directions? If your mirror is too small for you to see the entire room space, have someone watch you move to make sure you travel in all eight directions.

Combining Direction in Personal and General Space

Choose three directions, and picture them in your mind before you begin to move. Next, move both arms in the first direction by reaching both arms out as far as possible into your personal space. Then, walk in this same direction, going as far as you can in general space. Repeat the same process with the other two directions so that you move first in personal space, then travel in general space. Check the accuracy of your movements by looking in a mirror or by having someone watch you.

Levels in Space

It is possible to move at several different *levels*. If you are balanced on the balls of your feet, your body is moving at high level, whereas movements with the knees bent are at low level. Finally, moving with relatively straight knees places you at middle level, somewhere between the two extremes. In essence, you probably do much of your dancing at middle level because this is how you usually move in daily life. Middle level is, for most, a comfortable zone. Using space fully, however, means dancing at all three levels. Take some time to think about the dance steps you have learned in the past and decide whether you were dancing at high, middle, or low level. You may discover that you do some dance steps by moving through several levels (see figure 1.3).

FIGURE 1.3   Three basic levels.

Identifying Levels in Personal Space

Keep a picture in your mind of the three levels. Next, remain in one place and reach both arms away from your center so that you are extending them above your head, forward at waist level, and finally down toward the floor. As you move at the different levels, try to touch all the available space at each level. Check your movements in a mirror to determine whether you are really moving your arms at three different levels— high, middle, and low.

Moving at Different Levels in General Space

Go back to the image of three levels, and use this image to guide you as you walk throughout the entire room. Try to move through the whole room at each level. Look in a mirror, or have someone watch you walk to make sure you are moving at all three levels. Remember that you need to walk on three-quarter point at high level, with your feet flat on the floor at middle level, and with bent knees for low level.

Contrasting Levels

Choose an order for the levels at which you are going to do your movements. For example, you could move first at low level, then go to high level, and end at middle level. Then, use the order you have selected and move at each level in your personal space. Next, use the same order for movement level, and walk throughout the room in general space.

Straight Versus Curved Pathways

Pathways are the lines you trace in space when you move. You can trace pathways by moving one part of your body or by traveling across space with your whole body. Sometimes the pathways traced when you move your whole body are called floor patterns. In addition, spatial pathways can be straight or curved or a combination of the two. You can easily visualize spatial pathways by imagining that you are holding a paintbrush in your hand. Thus, if you hold the paintbrush right in front of your body and move your arm directly to the side and parallel to the floor, you will paint a straight path in space. On the other hand, starting from the same place and moving the paintbrush up, over to the side, and down will cause you to paint a curved pathway (see figure 1.4a-c). A similar image can be used to describe your path, or floor pattern, in general space. Here, you can imagine wet paint on the soles of your feet so that when you walk, you create a visible trail on the floor with your steps.

Identifying Pathways in Personal Space

Focus on the mental picture of a very straight path. Next, stand in one spot and, using a single direction and level, reach your arms out from your center by following a straight path as far as you can reach. Repeat the reaching action, but this time follow a curved path to the end point. This means that your arms will change level the second time you move. In this exploration it might also help to hold a flashlight in each hand and move in a dark room so that you can see the path traced by your movements. Again, watch your movements in a mirror. Does it look as though you are tracing a straight path and then a curved path in space as you perform each action?

Identifying Pathways in General Space

In this exploration, you will walk throughout the whole room, but this time you are guided by the mental picture of straight paths. Begin walking by using straight paths only. As you do this, you will find that you need to change direction as you near a wall or other object, so it may help to follow geometrically shaped paths such as a square or triangle. After you have walked through a floor pattern made of straight lines, switch to moving in a floor pattern that is made of curved lines. Here, you can imagine movement pathways such as circles, scallops, or even a figure eight. Again, check your floor patterns in a mirror, or have another person watch to determine whether you have followed first straight and then curved paths on the floor.

a

b

c

FIGURE 1.4a-c   A pathway in space.

Contrasting Pathways

Begin at one side of the room and walk along the longest straight path possible. Keep the location of this path in your mind, and walk along a second path that is curved and moves back and forth across the straight path. Then, draw a picture of each path.

Summary

You have explored all aspects of space in terms of where you can move. Where you move in space involves moving in your personal and general space and moving in different directions, at different levels, and on various paths. Take some time to challenge yourself and reflect on the different ways to move in space with the improvisation activity that follows.

Challenges and Reflections

Start and end this improvisation by moving in personal space. In between, walk throughout general space using at least three directions and two levels. Repeat the improvisation a second time, but change the order of the directions and levels you use in general space.

- Describe the pathways you used to travel throughout space. Were these pathways straight, curved, or a combination of the two?
- In what directions did you walk in general space?
- In what directions did you move in personal space?
- Describe the use of direction, level, and pathway in your favorite solution for this improvisation.
- Compare your use of direction, level, and pathway in personal space to the way you used each of these aspects in general space.

Moving With Purpose and Sensitivity

o you've moved from one end of a room to the other, around objects and in personal and general space. But did you notice *how* your body was moving? Say you reach out to shake someone's hand—you are using your arm and hand to reach out into space. But pretend that the person is too far away, so you have to lean forward to shake his hand, moving your whole body into space. In this example you have reached across personal space in two ways: by extending your hand and by leaning forward. If you step forward to shake this person's hand, you've also moved across general space (the space between you and the other person). As you note use of personal and general space, take time to discover how you might perform other actions that allow you to move in both kinds of space at the same time.

In this chapter, you will read about and work with what the body does while moving. You will look at the types of movements that different parts of your body can do. You will also work with isolations, which are movements involving only one body part at a time. How you support your body can also affect what your body is able to do while you move. Thus, you move differently when standing on one foot versus dancing on two feet. The shape in which you place your body plays an important part in what you do while you dance. A wide body shape, for instance, allows you to move with more freedom than a narrow body shape allows. Finally, you will look at two very different ways of moving your body: dancing in your personal space by using such actions as bending, stretching, and twisting (known as *nonlocomotor* movement) and dancing while you move across the floor in general space (called *locomotor* movement). Common locomotor actions are walking, running, and skipping.

Isolations and Leads

What your body does when you move is a result of the part of your body that moves and where movements happen. To understand this statement, think about how your body is put together. Your arm is made up of three separate parts, or segments. These segments are your hand, forearm, and upper arm. These three segments, in turn, are connected by joints, which permit specific types of movements. In your arm, the three joints are the wrist, elbow, and shoulder. Your hand can move up and down so that you bend and straighten your wrist. You know this action as a wave. Thus, the body part that moves is your hand, and the joint where the waving originates is your wrist.

The type of movement permitted in each joint of your body is somewhat different, however, so that there are different possibilities for movement in various joints. Let's look at your wrist again. The wrist allows movement up and down as you bend and straighten it, but you can do actions that go from side to side and diagonally as well. You can also trace a circle with your hand by connecting all the other movements that are possible in your wrist. Your elbow only lets you bend and straighten your arm; the shoulder provides many more movement possibilities. At your shoulder you can move your arm forward, backward, sideways, and diagonally. You can also twist in or out at your shoulder and trace a circular pathway with your arm in space. Taken together, the movement possibilities in the different joints of your body are front, back, side, and diagonal, plus inward and outward turning. In many joints it is also possible to trace a circular pathway by moving the body part in a circle.

The possibilities for movement at a particular joint depend on the structure of the joint. *Hinge, or uniaxial joints,* such as the elbow, only allow movement in two directions: bending and straightening. *Condyloid joints,* also known as *biaxial joints,* allow movement in four directions: bending and straightening and side-to-side shifting. The wrist is an example of a condyloid joint. *Triaxial joints,* also known as *ball and socket joints,* such as the shoulder and hip, not only let you bend and straighten the joint and go from side to side, but they also allow twisting. Such twisting actions are easier to understand if you think about a line that extends from the inside of your shoulder down the center of your arm. Then, you can visualize the twisting action as it occurs around this line.

When you stand in one place and move only one body part, you are doing an isolation. Isolations are an important part of jazz dance, but they occur in other dance forms as well. If you bend, straighten, or twist the joints of the arm, you are doing a simple isolation. It is also possible to do isolations in the center of your body. Such actions include shifting the ribs from side to side and tracing a circular path in space with your hips (see figure 2.1).

FIGURE 2.1   Isolations in the shoulder (top) and ribs (bottom).

When you dance, you may be expected to use isolations to lead your whole body into a movement. For instance, you can begin a movement sequence by taking your head forward; but if you move your head far enough in this direction, it will cause your whole body to move forward as well. Thus, the forward movement of your head leads your whole body into a forward action. It is also possible to use isolated movements of other body parts to lead into whole-body movements (see figure 2.2).

In the explorations that follow, you are again asked to position your body or move it in a specific way. You will also be expected to create a mental picture of each action before doing it and to check the accuracy of your movements by looking in a mirror or by having someone watch you as you move. A new element will be introduced in the following explorations, however, since you will be asked to focus on the body feelings that result from specific actions. The body feeling is how a movement feels in your body as you do it. For example, the wave described earlier would feel loose and rather floppy. In contrast, a punching action would feel more forceful and direct, a circling movement smooth, and so on.

Isolations in One Part of Your Body

Sit in a comfortable position on the floor with your legs out in front of your body. Then, pick a joint in your right arm and move your whole arm, lower arm, or hand in all the possible directions and pathways that you can think of. Now, choose another

FIGURE 2.2   Leading into a movement with different body parts.

joint in the same arm, and explore all the possible movement directions and pathways again. Each of the actions you have just done is an isolation, or a movement of a single body part at a single joint. End this exploration by repeating each isolation as you look in a mirror to make sure you are moving only one body part at a time. When you do the isolations, you should be able to feel each action in only one part of your body while the other body parts feel still.

Isolations in the Center of Your Body

Stand up and place your feet under your shoulders. Now, start to move in the center of your body by taking your ribs from side to side. Then, center your ribs again, and move them to the front, back, and diagonally. Look in a mirror to make sure you are moving only your ribs in the directions described. You should be able to feel these actions in your ribs while the rest of your body feels still. Explore some of the other movement possibilities in the center of your body. For example, try twisting your spine so that you turn your shoulders from one side of the room to the other. You can also move your center by bending and straightening your spine to the front, back, side, and diagonally.

Connecting Isolations With Whole Body Movements

Stand with your feet under your shoulders. Then, move one arm in whatever direction you like. Do not stop with the movement of your arm, but let the isolated action of your arm extend to your whole body so that your body travels in the same direction as your arm. As you perform this action, see a mental image of the movement as it begins in your arm and then extends into your body. Watch this movement in a mirror; it should look and feel as if the action begins in your arm and flows into your body.

Balance Versus Unbalanced Support

The way your body is supported can affect which body parts you are able to move. Think about moving while your body is supported in different ways. Of course, you usually dance on your feet, but it is possible to dance while you are sitting, kneeling, or lying on the floor. You might even like to be adventuresome and dance while you support your weight on your head. Thus, the part of your body that touches the floor acts as your base of support.

The way you support your body can make you feel stable or unstable. If you are seated, you will probably feel centered and balanced. But supporting your body on one foot provides a rather unstable base, making it difficult to balance. Your foot is a more unstable base because it is much smaller than the base you have while sitting. Changing level also changes how well your body is balanced or supported. Moving while seated is much more secure because your center is close to the floor. Moving while standing on one foot is less secure because your center is at a much higher level.

Balanced Versus Unbalanced Support in Personal Space

Sit on the floor with both legs crossed or straight in front of your body. Then, choose three isolated movements that you can do with one part of your body. Also make sure that you can do these movements while you are seated. Examples of such movements are twisting your arm at the shoulder or alternately lifting your right and left shoulders. The image you should have in your mind is one of stillness in your center with movement going on in your arms, head, or upper body. Next, stand up and balance on one foot. Again, do the same isolations you did while seated. This time, however, you should feel less balanced because your center is higher, and you are moving while supported on a smaller base. Have someone check your movements to make sure you are moving the selected body parts in isolation and supporting your body in the correct way.

Balanced Versus Unbalanced Support in General Space

This time lie on your belly with the palms of your hands by your head. Your legs are straight behind your body on the floor. Then, choose three directions and begin to move your body across space into each direction by pushing with your hands and toes against the floor. Have a clear picture of the directions in your mind and move as far as you can, first in one direction and then into the other two. This movement should feel very stable. Now, stand up and walk as far as you can in each direction, using the same order for the directions. Again, have a clear picture in your mind of each direction in space. Walking in the three directions should feel less stable because you are moving on a smaller base at a higher level. As you walk, you are transferring your base of support from one foot to the other as well. Transferring your weight from foot to foot should also feel less stable.

Combining Supports in Personal and General Space

Choose two ways you can support your body. However, one base of support should be large and low, and the other one should be small and high. Make sure that each type of base allows you to do movements in both personal and general space. Now, move in your personal space using both bases of support. Then, move in general space using both types of bases. Of course, when you move in personal space you will stay in one place, and when you move in general space you will travel throughout the room. Moving in personal space at a low level on a large base should feel the most balanced and secure. Traveling in general space at a high level using a small base will be the least secure and most unbalanced way of supporting your body.

Whole-Body Shapes

You can make many shapes with your whole body. You can stand with both arms extended above your shoulders so that you form a straight line. If you leave your arms above your head and move your upper body directly to the side, you will form a curved shape, much like the letter C. You can also use your whole body to make twisted shapes: Start by positioning your body in the curved shape. Then, use the upper part of your body to reach to the front or back and around (surrounding) the lower part of your body (see figure 2.3).

Whole-body shapes can also be narrow or wide. Thus, standing with your arms held tightly at your sides produces a narrow body shape, which takes up little space. In contrast, if you spread your feet apart and reach both arms out into your personal space, you make a wide shape with your whole body. A narrow body shape will feel much more confined than a wide body shape.

Finally, whole-body shapes can be balanced or unbalanced. If a body shape is balanced, the placement of each body part on the right side will mirror the placement of body parts on the left. If your body were made of paper, you could fold it in half and the two halves would be the same. In unbalanced body shapes, the placement on the two sides of your body does not match. Dancers usually call balanced body shapes *symmetrical* and unbalanced body shapes *asymmetrical*. It is also more difficult to balance the body while in asymmetrical body shapes (see figure 2.4).

FIGURE 2.3   Straight, curved, and twisted body shapes.

FIGURE 2.4   Symmetrical and asymmetrical body shapes.

Body Shapes in Personal Space

Stay in one spot and position your body so that you make a straight shape that is symmetrical. When you look at this shape in a mirror your body should form a straight line from one end to the other, and the right side of your body should match the left side. This body shape should also feel strong and direct. Second, make a curved body shape that is asymmetrical. Here, your body should describe a curved line from one end to the other, and the right side will not match the left side. The curved body shape should feel soft and rounded. Next, move from the curved body shape to one that is twisted and asymmetrical. When you check the twisted shape in the mirror you see that the upper part of your body is curved around, or surrounds, the lower part, and the right and left sides do not match. The twisted body shape should also produce a feeling of *opposition,* or pull, between the upper and lower halves of your body (see figure 2.5).

FIGURE 2.5   Other body shapes made in personal space.

Narrow Versus Wide Body Shapes in Personal Space

Repeat the straight, curved, and twisted body shapes you discovered in the preceding exploration. Remember that the straight shape is symmetrical and the curved and twisted shapes are asymmetrical. Now, make each of the three shapes as narrow and as wide as you can. Take time to compare the narrow and wide shapes in the mirror. It should be clear that the wide body shapes take up much more personal space than those that are narrow. The wide shapes should also feel large and expanded, whereas the narrow shapes feel confined.

Combining Body Shapes in General Space

Begin this exploration by using the straight, curved, and twisted body shapes you created in the first exploration in this section. Then, design a floor pattern you would like to use to move around general space. Next, decide where in this floor pattern you will use each of these three body shapes. Finally, move through the floor pattern, assuming each of the three body shapes at the appropriate place in the pattern. Have someone watch as you perform these movements to make sure you have followed the floor pattern and performed each shape accurately.

Nonlocomotor Movements

There are many ways you can move in your personal space. You can perform nonlocomotor movements with different parts of your body and by using various directions, levels, and paths in space. You have already done some nonlocomotor movements, such as bend and straighten. Other nonlocomotor movements include swing, sway, twist, turn, curl, stretch, sink, push, pull, and shake.

A *swing* involves moving a part of your body from side to side so that it goes through an *arc*, or curved path, in space. You can swing your arm from your shoulder or swing your leg from your hip. It is also possible to swing your whole body from your waist. *Swaying* involves taking the weight alternately from foot to foot so that your whole body goes from one side to the other. When you sway, the center of your body moves through a curved path in space. It is also possible to sway to the front and back and in diagonal directions. The swing and sway feel smooth and soft, and you should sense the change in direction as you repeat each of these actions.

Twisting is rotating one part of the body around a central axis while another part of the body continues to face in the original direction. For example, if you twist your spine, you can turn the top part of your body around the long line created by your spine while the bottom half of your body continues to face the direction of origin. To get a mental picture of a twisting action, think about twisting your body as if it were a towel that you twist by holding it at each end. You should be able to feel tension across the front of your body as you twist. A *turn* involves rotating the whole body around an axis. Turns can be a quarter, half, three-quarter, and full rotation of the body (see figure 2.6a-d). Turns feel smooth until you stop the motion of the turn (put on the brakes).

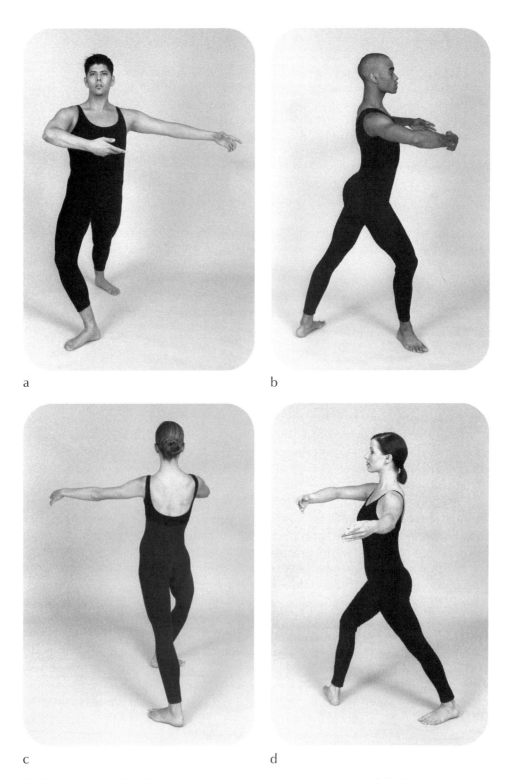

a

b

c

d

FIGURE 2.6a-d   The dancers have stopped turning to produce full, three-quarter, half, and quarter turns, respectively.

In a *bend,* you narrow the space between two connecting body segments so that they come closer together. Thus, when you bend your elbow, you do so by bringing your forearm closer to your upper arm. You can also bend in the spine by closing the space between your upper and lower body halves. A *curl* is an extreme form of bending. To curl your body down to the floor, lower the top half of your body and hold it very close to the lower part of your body. It is also possible to curl the upper and lower halves of your body so close together that your body resembles a ball. The end result of bending and curling should feel rather confined.

Straightening is the opposite of bending; to straighten a joint means to open the space between two connected parts of the body. You can straighten one body part or your whole body. To *stretch* is to reach a part of your body away from your center. For example, you may need to stretch to reach an object on a high shelf. Straightening and stretching should feel expanded and open. *Sinking* means taking your body or a part of your body to a lower level. When you perform a sinking action, your body should feel as though it is growing heavier.

Push and *pull* are opposite actions that can occur in one part of the body or in the whole body. To visualize pushing, imagine that you are pressing a heavy object away from your body. Pulling would involve bringing the same heavy object toward your body. When you do a pushing or pulling action, you should feel tension throughout your whole body.

Shaking is making a part of your body or your whole body vibrate in space. Shaking movements feel tense, but the tension is more intermittent than a pushing or pulling action.

Nonlocomotor Movements With One Body Part

Choose three of the nonlocomotor movements you have just read about. See each of these actions in your mind. Then, do each action with one arm. Next, turn toward a mirror and repeat the same three movements. The movements you see in the mirror should resemble the picture you have in your mind. Describe how each of these actions felt in your body. Finally, do the same three nonlocomotor movements with another part of your body, and again think about how each movement felt in your body.

Nonlocomotor Movements With the Whole Body

This time choose three nonlocomotor movements that you can do with your whole body. Again, see each of these actions in your mind. Then, stand in one spot and do each of the movements using your whole body. Check all of the actions in a mirror, and take time to focus on how each one feels in your body.

Choose three nonlocomotor actions, but make sure you can do each action with one body part as well as with your whole body. Some examples of such movements are twisting your arm at the shoulder and twisting your whole body, and bending your arm and bending your back. Try to use a different part of your body from the body part you used in the first exploration in this section. If you used your right arm in the earlier exercise, use your left arm or one of your legs this time. Begin by doing the first movement in a specific direction, but use only one part of your body. Now use your whole body, and repeat the same action you just did; but this time change its direction. Perform the other nonlocomotor movements you selected, doing each with one body part, followed by the same movement with your whole body but in a different direction.

Locomotor Movements

Locomotor movements take place in general space; they move your body from one point to another. Think about the many ways in which you can move across space. You walk every day, but other actions such as running, hopping, jumping, skipping, sliding, galloping, leaping, and turning can carry you through space as well. Walking, running, hopping, jumping, and leaping are even movements because each part of these steps takes the same amount of time. Skipping, sliding, and galloping are uneven because these steps have two parts that take up different amounts of time. For example, a skip consists of a step and a hop, with the step taking more time than the hop. The skip could be described with the words *long* for the step and *short* for the hop.

In a *walk*, the most basic of the even locomotor movements, one foot is always on the ground. As you step off on one foot, the other foot must come down on the floor. *Running* is similar to walking because you push off with alternate feet. Running occurs at a faster pace than walking, and there is a point at which both feet are off the ground. In a run, the center of the body follows a path in space that looks like a series of small arcs.

Hops and *jumps* both go into the air and land, except in a hop you land on one foot and in a jump you land on two feet. In both of these locomotor moves you must bend your knees on the push-off and on the landing. A leap is a larger, higher version of a run. You must use more force on the push-off and reach the lead leg farther out into the direction of the leap. *Turns* can be both a nonlocomotor and a locomotor movement.

The *skip*, the first of the uneven locomotor movements, is made up of a step and a hop performed on alternating feet. In a *slide*, your feet glide across the floor and move through wide and narrow positions as you travel sideways. As you pull your feet into the narrow position, you push your body into the air. Then, you land on one foot with your legs close together, separating them again in preparation for the next slide. While you do a slide, the center of your body traces a path

FIGURE 2.7   Two phases of a slide: preparation (left) and push-off into air (right).

that is a series of upside-down arcs in space (see figure 2.7). Galloping is simply a slide done to the front rather than to the side.

Even Locomotor Movements

Review the description of the even locomotor movements: walk, run, hop, jump, and leap. Then, pick two of these steps and picture yourself in your mind as you do each one. Next, create a simple floor pattern that can carry you around the room in general space. This floor pattern should include both straight and curved paths. Finally, follow the floor pattern you created using the two even locomotor movements you selected.

Have someone watch you as you perform the two traveling steps to make sure you are doing them correctly. The two locomotor moves should also feel different in your body. For instance, a walk feels long and low in comparison to a run, and a jump feels more stable than a hop because you are landing on two feet in a jump. Describe how each locomotor step feels in your body.

Uneven Locomotor Movements

Reread the description of the uneven locomotors: skip, slide, and gallop. Then, choose two of these moves, and picture yourself in your mind as you perform them. Next, do the two locomotor moves throughout the room, but do each at a different level. To check your accuracy, someone should watch you as you do the two locomotor moves. End this exploration by thinking about how each locomotor movement felt in your body as you did it.

Combining Even and Uneven Locomotor Movements

Choose two even locomotor steps and one that is uneven. Then, use the whole room to go from one locomotor move to another. Use curved paths when you are doing the even locomotor moves and straight paths for the uneven locomotor moves.

Summary

You have explored ways to move your body—by moving one part in isolation or with movements of your whole body. The type of movements you can do are determined by the body part involved. You have also explored how body shapes can affect the type of movements you can do, all of which affect your balance. You have worked with locomotor and nonlocomotor movements as well. By practicing these types of actions, you can create moves in your own style. Now challenge yourself and reflect on these concepts in the improvisation activity that follows.

Challenges and Reflections

Begin this improvisation with a symmetrical body shape, and end it with an asymmetrical body shape. Travel around the room using three different locomotor movements while alternating body shapes. During the traveling part of this sequence, stop at two points. The first time you stop, do a nonlocomotor movement using one body part. During the second stop, assume a position in which you are supporting your body on a very small base. Repeat this improvisation using different types of beginning and ending shapes and three other locomotor moves. In the second improvisation, you might want to change the way you support your body, and perform another nonlocomotor action.

- Describe where you put different parts of your body in your personal space to make the beginning and ending shapes in each improvisation. Then, draw some comparisons between the different shapes.
- Describe each of the shapes you created.

- What part of your body did you use to do the nonlocomotor movement in each improvisation? Can you do this nonlocomotor action with another part of your body?
- What part of your body did you use to support yourself in each improvisation? Was it difficult or easy to balance when you supported your body in this way?
- Compare your use of movement in personal space with the movements you used in general space throughout each improvisation.
- Compare your use of directions, levels, and pathways in each improvisation.
- Describe some of the body feelings you experienced in each improvisation.

chapter 3

Balancing Time and Energy

Y ou know about the space around you and how to create moves within that space. Now we're going to focus on creating a balance of time and energy with those movements. Think about the way in which your use of energy determines how your body moves. If you use a lot of energy to propel your actions, your movements are bold and forceful. In contrast, using very little energy makes your movements soft and much more timid. Using energy in contrasting ways is called *dynamics.*

How the body moves can be described in several ways. We talk about the *tempo,* or speed, at which an action is performed. For example, you can bend your elbow in 1 second, but bending your elbow very slowly may take as long as 10 seconds. *Quality* refers to the way you use energy when you do a movement. In this chapter, you will look at quality in two ways. First, you explore contrasts in quality: light versus heavy energy. Then, you experience six movement qualities so that you know how these qualities feel in your own body. The six energy qualities are sustained, percussive, vibratory, swinging, suspended, and collapsed. In the last section of this chapter, rhythm and rhythmic patterns are the basis of your explorations.

Dynamics of Movement

Dynamics refer to the forces that cause your body to move in various ways. Energy is used to put your body into motion when you are still and to change the quality or speed of your actions when you are already moving. When we compare different ways of using energy in the body we are talking about dynamics. In music, dynamics are the loudness and softness of sound. Movements can be loud or soft as well when you use energy in different ways. Thus, a loud movement is bold and requires more energy, whereas a soft movement is less forceful and requires less energy to perform. Fast movements like running and jumping also need more energy to propel the body through space.

SLOW VERSUS FAST SPEED

The speed of a movement can vary a great deal. Let's use a reaching action as an example. One way to determine the speed of the reach is to count how many seconds it takes to complete the action. Another method for estimating reaching speed is to use counts. Thus, a reach completed in two counts is certainly faster than a reaching action that lasts for eight counts.

In each of the preceding examples—timing the reaching action and counting it—speed is determined by relating the performance of the reach to a measure or unit of time. It is possible to say that a regular time interval was established in relation to the performance of the reach. Once you establish the time interval, you measure the speed by counting the number of intervals it takes to complete the reach. Counting time intervals is also what you do when you dance with music. Music is based on a regular time interval called a *beat,* or *pulse.* Consequently, a slow action requires more beats of music than a fast movement requires.

Slow Versus Fast Speed in Personal Space

Choose one of the nonlocomotor actions you explored in chapter 2. Remember that nonlocomotor actions are movements such as bending, twisting, and stretching. Second, decide which part of your body you would like to use to do the nonlocomotor action. Then, find a position in which you can move this body part easily. If you decide to move your arm, you might like to stand. If you choose to move your leg in a leg lift, however, lying on the floor allows more freedom for movement. Make sure you can see the second hand on a clock from where you are located in the room, or ask a partner to time you. Now, perform the action you selected, and do it as fast as you can. Count the number of seconds it takes to do this movement quickly. Repeat the same action, but this time do it as slowly as possible. Count the number of seconds it takes to do the movement slowly. Finally, do the same movement at an intermediate speed, timing the movement as you do it. Compare the time it takes to do the same action at fast, slow, and intermediate speeds. Watch in a mirror as you do the same action at the three different speeds. The same movement done at three different speeds should look different as well. Performing the same action at three different speeds also feels different in your body. For example, the fast action should feel tense in comparison to a more relaxed feeling that goes with slow movement. To end this exploration, challenge yourself by doing the same nonlocomotor action at three different speeds in three different parts of your body to create a short movement sequence.

Slow Versus Fast Speed in General Space

Begin by picking one of the locomotor movements you explored in chapter 2. Remember that locomotor movements include walking, running, hopping, jumping, skipping, sliding, leaping, and galloping. Turns that move across space are also locomotor movements. Now, perform the selected locomotor movement in general space in a floor pattern that describes a circle with a large S inside of it. As you repeat this floor pattern, move at a moderate pace, then at a fast pace, and then at a slow pace. Ask someone to watch you do this sequence to make sure it is obvious that you are performing the locomotor movement at three different speeds. Did you find that you had a preferred speed for doing this movement? Why do you think that you liked doing the movement at this speed? Now, challenge yourself by doing a movement sequence that includes two or three locomotor movements performed at three different speeds.

Combining Slow and Fast Movements

In this exploration you will do a nonlocomotor action with one arm while you use your legs to travel throughout space. Begin by selecting an even locomotor step such as walking or running. Then, do this locomotor move throughout general space, covering as much area as possible. The locomotor step you perform is the interval, or beat, that serves as a basis for timing this exploration. Now, choose a nonlocomotor action that you can do with one arm while you perform the locomotor step you just practiced. For example, you can swing one arm to the front and back while you walk. Do the nonlocomotor action more slowly than the locomotor step. If you do one arm swing for every three walking steps, you are swinging your arm more slowly than you are walking. But doing two arm swings for each walking step means that you are moving your arm faster than your legs. After you have practiced the nonlocomotor and locomotor movements together, have someone watch you to make sure that there is a difference in the speed at which you perform the two actions. Finally, challenge yourself by swinging your arm faster than the speed at which you are walking.

LIGHT VERSUS HEAVY FORCE

The terms *light* and *heavy* refer to the quality, or use of energy, in a movement. A light movement requires a small amount of energy in comparison to a heavy action. Light actions can also be described as delicate in comparison to the more powerful force needed for heavy actions. For example, if you move your arm as if it were a feather floating to the floor, you use a small amount of energy in a delicate way. If you move your arm as if you were pushing a large, heavy rock, you use lots of energy. Pushing a large, heavy rock also takes considerable strength. If you think about the body feelings that accompany each of these actions, you should discover that floating feels light and pushing feels heavy.

Light Versus Heavy Force in Personal Space

Stand in one spot and select a nonlocomotor movement that you can do with one body part. Also choose an action and a part of your body that you have not used before. Now, do your selected nonlocomotor movement with a light use of energy. You should feel as if you are pushing a light gauze curtain aside with your body part. Repeat the same nonlocomotor movement, but do it with heavy energy. This time you should feel as if you are pushing a heavy piece of furniture. Next, watch in a mirror as you do the nonlocomotor movement with light and then heavy energy. The light movement should look gentle, whereas the heavy action appears more forceful. The light movement also should feel more relaxed than the heavy action.

Light Versus Heavy Force in General Space

Pick a different locomotor step than those you used in the earlier explorations in this chapter. Perform this step in general space, attempting to travel throughout the room. Next, do this same locomotor move again, but do it with a light use of energy. Conclude this exploration by performing the same locomotor movement with heavy energy. Have a partner check your performance of the light and heavy locomotor moves. Performing the locomotor movement in these two ways should look different to an observer. In particular, doing the locomotor movement with heavy energy should look as if it is more difficult and requires more work. The two versions of the locomotor moves should also feel different in your body. Which way of doing the locomotor movement did you like the best? Why do you think that you liked to do the locomotor movement in this way?

Combining Light and Heavy Actions

Begin this exploration by walking throughout the general space while moving both arms at the same time. You should find that you can move your arms forward, backward, sideways, and diagonally. Once you practice walking while moving your arms, walk and move your arms as if you are pushing a very heavy object. Bending your knees while you walk also helps you move in a heavy way. Focus on using other parts of your body such as your hips or back, and imagine that you are using these body parts to help push the heavy object. After you perfect your heavy walk, practice a light walk and move your arms as lightly as you can at the same time. Imagine that your upper body is a feather floating in the air and that you are using your lower body to part a curtain made of lightweight material. Now, combine the heavy and light actions in one movement sequence by moving your arms in a light way above a heavy walk in the lower part of your body. Again, have someone watch you to make sure your walk looks heavy and your upper body looks delicate and light. The lower part of your body should, of course, feel much more tense than your upper body.

FREE VERSUS BOUND FLOW

Free and *bound flow* also refer to the way in which you use energy in your body. Free-flow movements look abandoned and carefree and appear uncontrolled. It is not possible to stop free-flow movements quickly. Floppy movement is a good example of free flow. To better understand this type of energy quality, imagine that you are holding a rag doll in one hand. If you hold the doll by the legs and twist it from side to side, its arms will move in a way that is floppy and uncontrolled. Shaking out a dusty blanket is a good example of an everyday movement that is done in free flow.

Movements in bound flow have a more restricted use of energy and are easy to stop because they are more controlled. The actions of a tightrope walker are a good example of bound flow, as is the act of writing on a blackboard or on a piece of paper. When a person moves in bound flow, he is ready to stop so that he can change or adjust the movement.

Free-flow movements feel relaxed, whereas bound actions feel more tense. It is also easier to do free-flow movements that are light and bound flow actions that are heavy. You can draw some other relationships between light, heavy, free, and bound uses of energy as well. For example, doing free-flow movements in a heavy way restricts the freedom of such actions. It is also possible to perform bound movements with both light and heavy energies. Thus, you can write with a light touch and with a heavy use of energy.

Free Versus Bound Flow in Personal Space

Stand in one spot and do a nonlocomotor movement with one part of your body. Do this movement at three different levels without stopping between level changes. Then, do the same nonlocomotor movement at all three levels, alternately using both free and bound flow. The action in free flow should look loose and floppy in the mirror, and the bound action should appear more controlled and restrained. In terms of body feeling, the free-flow action should feel relaxed and careless, whereas the bound action should feel tense and precise.

Free Versus Bound Flow in General Space

Walk around in general space in a very loose, relaxed manner. If you are doing a free-flow walk, your arms and legs move in several directions and feel relaxed. To an observer, it looks as if you are unsure about the direction of your walking; your walk looks hesitant. Now, change the quality of your walk to bound flow. When you walk in bound flow, your movements should look precise—there's no question about the direction in which you are walking. Again, have someone watch you walk in these two ways to make sure that your free-flow walk looks relaxed and carefree and your bound walk looks controlled.

Combining Free-Flow and Bound Movements

In this exploration, you perform actions that use free flow in one part of your body and bound flow in another part of your body. An example of using free and bound flow at the same time is drawing a circle on the floor with one foot while you shake one arm. To start this exploration, stand in one spot and do a nonlocomotor movement with one leg using bound flow. Keep this action going and do another nonlocomotor movement with one arm using free flow. Your leg should be very controlled while your arm is relaxed and floppy. Look in a mirror to check whether you are doing controlled movements with your leg and loose, floppy movements with your arm. Your arm should feel relaxed and free while your leg feels tense and controlled. Choose two other body parts and move them using free flow in one body part and bound flow in the other one.

Qualities of Movement

We've explored the two energy qualities and contrasted them in movement explorations. Now we will explore the six movement qualities that use energy in a variety of ways.

SUSTAINED

In *sustained* movements, the dancer moves smoothly and with a continuous flow of energy. Sustained movement is very controlled. As with movements done in bound flow, sustained actions can be stopped easily at any point in the action. Sustained movements do not have points of emphasis, or accents, so it is hard to tell where such actions begin and end. Sustained movements can occur in one body part or in the whole body.

PERCUSSIVE

The use of energy in *percussive* movements contrasts with the energy use in sustained actions. Percussive movements are explosive and hard-hitting. Such actions also have a definite beginning and ending and are propelled with sharp thrusts of energy. Percussive movements trace a straight, direct pathway in space. It is easier to perform percussive movements with one body part than it is to do them with the whole body. Many of the movements in karate are percussive. (See figure 3.1.)

VIBRATORY

Vibratory movement produces shaking actions. To the observer, vibratory movements look jittery and nervous; and if a percussive movement is done very fast, it turns into a vibratory movement. Vibratory movements can occur in one body part or in the whole body. Stretching a rubber band and plucking it in the stretched position produces a vibratory action.

FIGURE 3.1   Percussive movement.

SWINGING

When you do *swinging* movements, you allow your body to relax and give in to gravity on the downward part of the swing. To finish a swing you need to use energy to pull away from gravity to move upward. Thus, a swing traces a curved pathway in space. You can perform swinging movements with your arm at your shoulder and with your leg at your hip. You can also swing your head at your neck and your upper body at your waist. It is easier to swing shorter body parts at a faster speed, although there is a point at which a swing becomes so fast that it turns into a vibratory movement. Vibratory and swinging actions can be repetitive as well.

SUSPENDED

Suspended movements hover in space momentarily and appear to defy gravity. When you leap, you are suspended for an instant at the highest point of this movement. Dancers also suspend when they are poised for action before moving across space. Suspended movements can occur in one part of the body and in the whole body. (See figure 3.2.)

COLLAPSED

Collapsing actions also involve giving in to the pull of gravity. When you collapse, you release tension from your body and become more relaxed by the end of the movement. A collapse can occur at a slow or fast speed. In a slow collapse, you resist gravity and your body feels as if it melts to the floor. A fast collapse gives you a dropping sensation. It is possible to use your whole body or a single body part to do a collapse. (See figure 3.3.)

FIGURE 3.2   Suspended movement.   FIGURE 3.3   Collapsing movement.

Using Movement Qualities in Personal Space

Select two nonlocomotor movements. Next, use one body part, and then your whole body, to do each nonlocomotor action. For example, you can reach into personal space with just your arm and with your whole body. Finally, use one body part and then your whole body to perform the same two nonlocomotor movements using energy in two different ways. You can reach one arm using both sustained and vibratory movements. You can also reach with your whole body using sustained and vibratory energies. Did you find one of the movements easier for you? Why do you think this movement was easier?

Using Movement Qualities in General Space

Choose a single locomotor movement. Then, use this movement to travel around general space, and make sure that your floor pattern contains both straight and curved paths. Next, use the same floor pattern and the same locomotor movement, but change your energy quality at three places in the floor pattern. Compare your ability to do the locomotor movement using the three different energies. Which energy quality was easier for you to do?

Combining Nonlocomotor and Locomotor Movements

Put together a movement sequence that contains three nonlocomotor movements and two locomotor movements. Then, practice this movement sequence so that you can perform it from beginning to end without stopping. Next, perform the whole sequence two times—once using sustained movement, and a second time using percussive energy. Compare the body feelings you experience when you do this movement sequence using the two different energies. Finally, do the same movement sequence a second time using a third energy quality. Which energy quality was easiest for you to perform?

Creating Rhythmic Patterns

In chapter 2, you practiced two types of locomotor movements—those that were even and others that were uneven. Remember that in even locomotor movements each part takes the same amount of time as the part before or after it. Uneven locomotor movements have one part that lasts for a longer time than another part. This is the case with a skip, because the step in a skip takes more time than the hop.

The point here is that the two types of locomotor movements create two types of rhythmic patterns. In even rhythmic patterns, each separate action takes the same amount of time. In uneven patterns, there is a difference in the amount of time it takes to do each part of the pattern. The idea of uneven rhythms can apply to longer sequences of movement as well. For instance, you can do a movement sequence made up of four walking steps and two skips. This produces a movement sequence in which the rhythm is four even beats followed by slow and quick beats repeated two times. Figure 3.4 represents the overall pattern for this movement sequence. In this figure, the four dashes of equal length stand for the four walking steps, and each grouping of long and short dashes represents a skip.

FIGURE 3.4   Rhythmic pattern made up of even and uneven locomotors.

Rhythmic patterns are not limited to locomotor steps, however. It is possible to do the rhythmic pattern shown in figure 3.4 with nonlocomotor movements. You can bend one arm intermittently until it is in a fully bent position so that each part of the bending action takes the same amount of time. This means that you are performing the bending action in an even rhythm to duplicate the action depicted in the four equal dashes in the first part of the figure. Then, you can straighten your arm using the uneven rhythms to reproduce the second part of the pattern. Thus, you do four separate movements to straighten your arm, but these four actions are performed in the pattern of slow, quick, slow, quick.

At this point, you should realize that an uneven rhythmic pattern is created when you move at varying speeds within a single movement sequence. Consequently, a movement sequence that includes two walking steps and three running steps forms another rhythmic pattern. This pattern can be described as slow, slow, quick, quick, quick.

Even Versus Uneven Rhythms with Nonlocomotor Movements

Choose a different body part and a different nonlocomotor movement than you used in the previous explorations in this chapter. Draw a diagram of a short rhythmic pattern that is no more than eight counts long, making one part of this rhythmic pattern even and the other part uneven. Perform your selected nonlocomotor movement following the rhythmic pattern you created. Check your performance of this pattern in a mirror to make sure the even parts take the same amount of time and the uneven parts take different amounts of time. The even part of the rhythmic pattern should feel regular and steady in your body, and the uneven part of the pattern should feel more irregular and erratic.

Even Versus Uneven Rhythms with Locomotor Movements

Choose two different locomotor movements from those you used earlier in this chapter. One of these movements should be even, and the other one should be uneven. Again, draw a diagram of a short rhythmic pattern that is eight counts long. Make sure that this pattern is divided into even and uneven parts that are based on the two selected locomotor movements. Use the even locomotor movement to perform the even part of the pattern and the uneven locomotor to perform the uneven part of the pattern. Perform this pattern several times, and have someone watch you. It should be clear that you are doing both even and uneven rhythms and that you are reproducing the entire rhythmic pattern accurately. The even locomotor movement should feel regular, whereas the uneven one should feel more sporadic. Challenge yourself by varying the even and uneven locomotor movements within a new eight-count rhythmic pattern, perhaps alternating each locomotor movement every two counts or less.

Combining Nonlocomotor and Locomotor Movements

Draw a new diagram that represents a rhythmic pattern that lasts for 16 counts. As you create the diagram of this pattern, decide where you want to do nonlocomotor movements and where you want to include locomotor movements. Also decide on the specific nonlocomotor and locomotor moves you want to do. Next, perform the entire rhythmic pattern several times. Have someone watch you to make sure you are doing each part of the rhythmic pattern accurately and that the pattern includes both nonlocomotor and locomotor actions. Challenge yourself to do the same pattern using other nonlocomotor and locomotor movements.

Summary

Movement is all about time and energy. Your movements may be fast or slow, choppy or graceful, depending on the type of energy you expend. That energy can be described in six qualities—sustained, percussive, vibratory, swinging, suspended, and collapsed. Changing the timing of your movements also creates rhythms. Think about these concepts as you try out the improvisation exercise that follows.

Challenges and Reflections

Select any locomotor movement that moves you throughout space. Next, choose several nonlocomotor movements that you can do in your upper body above the moving base. Then, begin traveling at a high level using free-flow actions, and end with low and bound movements. As you travel, make a gradual transition from high to low and from free to bound flow. Do the same nonlocomotor and locomotor movements throughout space. This time, however, begin at a low level with heavy movements, and end at a high level using light actions.

- Think about the first movement sequence you just performed, and describe which parts of your body you used throughout the sequence. Was it easier to do the free-flow movements in the upper or lower part of your body? What about your ability to do the bound movements in the different parts of your body? How did the level affect your performance of the movements?

- Describe the speed of your actions in each part of the first movement sequence. Was there a relationship between free-flow or bound movements and their speeds? What about the relationship between high- or low-level movements and their speeds?

- Draw a diagram of the rhythmic patterns you performed throughout the first movement sequence. Indicate in the diagram where the rhythms were even and where they were uneven.

- Compare your ability to do the first movement sequence to your ability to do the second sequence. Was one sequence easier for you? If so, why do you think this was so?

chapter

4

Relating to People and Objects

We have explored where the body travels in space, what you do as you move, and how movements are performed. You have performed these movements alone, but now it's time to challenge yourself further and think about those concepts in terms of dancing in relation to other dancers and objects on the stage. When you perform, you must be aware of where objects and other dancers are located onstage. Think about the times you danced as part of a group or ensemble. Perhaps it was important to keep equal spacing between dancers in the group. Or your role might have been to travel between or around other dancers or objects.

Relationships among dancers and between dancers and objects onstage are an important part of performing. In this chapter you will explore many of these relationships. For example, dancers frequently move and relate to objects onstage, such as chairs and stage sets. Relationships among dancers exist if you perform with a partner or as part of a group. Each of these types of relationships is explored in a separate section of this chapter.

Relating to Objects

It is possible to establish spatial relationships with objects onstage. These objects include various props and stage sets. Dance props are usually rather small, but sets can be quite large and take up a lot of space onstage. Chairs, scooters, hoops, and streamers are examples of props used in a dance (see figure 4.1). Props such as chairs are larger and more difficult to move, however, so it is usually the dancer who does the moving in relation to the prop. You can move around, in front of, behind, and beside a chair. It is also possible for you to move across or get on or off a chair by sitting or standing on it. If more than one chair is onstage, you can move between the chairs as well. Smaller, lighter props such as a scarf or a hoop can be moved more easily, so such props are manipulated in space to create relationships with dancers. In other words, with smaller props, the prop itself is moved to create various dancer–prop relationships. You can swirl a scarf in front of, behind, above, below, and at the side of your body. You can even move a scarf around your body and between body parts, such as between your legs.

Dancers can create the same spatial relationships with stage sets as they do with props. Imagine that the set is a large arch that takes up a lot of space onstage. You can move in front of, behind, beside, around, and under this set. If the set is a large platform, however, you can also move on or across it.

Relating to Fluid Objects That Change Shape

Find a small prop that you can move easily and that changes shape as you move it. A good example of such a prop is a scarf or long ribbon. Practice moving this prop around in space so that you can learn how it moves. Then, explore by moving this prop at two levels and in three directions. Begin by staying in one spot, moving in your personal space. Then, extend this exploration by traveling throughout space. After you complete this exploration, describe the relationships you created between your body and the prop.

FIGURE 4.1   Various props used in dance.

You may have moved the prop over, around, and beside your body. What about the pathways you created with the prop in space? Were these pathways straight, curved, or a combination of the two?

Relating to Rigid Objects

The object in this exploration is a chair. Find a chair that is large enough to support your weight and is stable so that you can get on and off of it easily. Place this chair in the middle of your movement space. Next, create five shapes with your body. Two of these shapes should be balanced, and three should be unbalanced. Decide how you are going to position each body shape so that the shape of your body forms a spatial relationship to the chair. Remember that it is possible to position or move your body in front of, behind, beside, above, and below the chair. You can also move through parts of the chair. Move continuously from one shape to the next after you have found a place for each body shape in relationship to the chair.

Object Relationships in Personal and General Space

Begin by standing next to the same chair you used in the previous exploration. Choose three ways you can move in relation to the chair. For example, moving around, over, and beside are three ways you can move and relate to the chair. Now, select a nonlocomotor movement and a locomotor movement that you can use to relate to the chair in the three ways you selected. You can reach around the chair and walk around the chair. First, practice the nonlocomotor movement and locomotor movement by relating to the chair in all three ways. Then, repeat each of the movements using the three ways of relating to the chair, but change your use of energy so that if a movement was sustained it becomes percussive, and so on. Finally, repeat each of your movement relationships again, but this time change your use of time. Was it easy or difficult to make the changes in energy? What about the difficulty with the changes in timing? Why do you think that some of the changes in movement quality and timing were more difficult than others?

Relating to a Partner

Dancing with a partner brings other relationship possibilities into play. It may mean that one person is the leader and the other person is the follower. The dancer doing the leading, of course, is the dancer who initiates the movements, while the follower copies the leader's actions. The follower can also respond to the leader's movements rather than simply copy them. For example, if the leader travels forward, the follower can respond by traveling backward. It is also possible for the leader and the follower to exchange roles (see figure 4.2).

A second aspect of dancing with a partner involves meeting and parting. When you meet your partner, you approach the other person and then continue to

FIGURE 4.2 Following and responding.

dance closely. A good example of meeting your partner is to approach and come together in a couple dance position. You and your partner can continue to dance in this position. Parting is the opposite of meeting; it involves moving away from your partner so that you and your partner are no longer close together.

The last partner relationship is mirroring. In mirroring, one dancer is again the leader, but the other dancer performs actions that are a mirror image of the leader's movements. When you mirror the actions of another dancer, you move as though you are looking into a full-length mirror. Thus, in mirroring the follower does each action on the opposite side of her body. Mirroring works best if the leader's movements are simple and slow. Complicated movements and fast actions tend to break the level of concentration between the two dancers. Turning your back to your partner can also destroy the concentration between you and your partner. (See figure 4.3.)

Leading and Following

Begin working with a partner by deciding who will be the leader and who will be the follower. Stand so that the leader is in front of and close to the follower with both dancers facing the same direction. The leader begins to move when he feels ready. The follower copies the leader's actions, taking care to reproduce the leader's movements accurately in terms of where, what, and how the leader is moving. Also use sustained movements so that the follower can copy the movements easily. Leaders who have problems creating movements can think about the types of actions possible at different joints in the body. As you explore, remember that some joints have a

FIGURE 4.3   Mirroring.

greater potential for movement than others. Stay focused on the leader's actions. Remember to trade places so that each partner has a chance to play both roles. One way to change roles is for the leader to freeze in a body shape to communicate that he is ready to give the leadership to the other dancer. Have someone watch you throughout the leading and following exercise to make sure the follower is accurately copying the leader's movements. It helps to play slow, sustained music as you do this exploration.

Meeting and Parting

Begin this exploration by facing a partner and standing on opposite sides of the room. Walk forward, and gradually approach each other. When you are close to your partner, continue to move by walking once around in a circle with your partner. After completing one circle, separate and walk off in the opposite direction. Thus, you and your partner will follow a specific pathway made up of a straight line, a circle, and another straight line. After you and your partner have practiced meeting and parting, do this movement sequence again, but this time change the timing at various points. For example, you and your partner could move toward each other rapidly, circle slowly, and exit rapidly. Another variation is to enter slowly, circle rapidly, and exit slowly. Have someone watch to determine whether the floor patterns you and your partner follow are a straight line, a circle, and another straight line. You and your partner should also feel a stronger connection as you approach and a weakening relationship as you part. The person observing should be able to sense the contrasting feeling from this movement sequence when you and your partner perform it with the changes in timing. Challenge yourself by using other floor patterns that involve meeting your partner and then parting.

Mirroring

Stand facing your partner so that there is a comfortable distance between your bodies. Decide who the leader is and who the follower is. The leader begins to move when she is ready. The follower's job is to mirror the leader's movements. This means that when the leader moves on the left, the follower moves on the right. It is also important for the leader to move slowly and use simple actions. The partners should face each other throughout and restrict their movements to the personal space surrounding their bodies. Using simple actions, continuing to face each other, and staying in one spot improve the focus between the two dancers. Thinking about the movement potential at different joints or about a variety of nonlocomotor movements also helps the leader come up with new actions in this situation. The leader can also extend this exploration by changing the direction, level, pathway, timing, and energy quality of the selected movements. It helps to play slow, sustained music as you do this exploration.

Relating in a Group

Imagine that you are moving onstage with a group of dancers. You may be asked to stay in the same place within the group and maintain a constant relationship with them, but this is usually not the case. Instead, the choreographer will most likely move dancers around onstage to create a series of changing relationships, because change is more interesting for the audience to watch. As a dancer, you might be expected to move between or through other dancers. You may also be asked to travel inside, outside, or across the group; or you may follow a floor pattern that takes you around another dancer or dancers. Other possibilities are moving in front, behind, or side by side with other dancers in the ensemble. If dancers are positioned at different levels, you can even dance above or below the other performers (see figure 4.4).

Group Relationships in Personal Space

Begin by standing close to your partner but not touching him. Have your partner put his body in an interesting shape. It is your job to move and relate to the shape made by your partner's body. You can do this by moving over, under, beside, around, and through your partner's body shape. Remember, however, that you are moving in personal space only, so you need to stay in one spot as you move. Finally, extend this exploration by moving at different speeds and with different energy qualities as you relate to the shape of your partner's body. You can begin this exploration anew by having your partner assume a new body shape at a different level from the first body shape.

FIGURE 4.4 Relationships among dancers.

Group Relationships in General Space

Have your partner draw a diagram of a floor pattern that fills the whole space in which you are moving. This floor pattern can include straight and curved paths. Watch as your partner moves through the floor pattern she created. Next, have your partner perform the same floor pattern again. This time, however, you are going to move in a relationship with your partner. You can move in front of, behind, or beside your partner parallel to her. You can also move toward or away from your partner or from one side of your partner to the other. You might even like to move above and below or circle around your partner. Try to explore all the possibilities in this situation. Which movement relationships were the easiest for you to perform? Which ones were the most difficult? Why do you think that some of the movement relationships were easy and others were more difficult?

Multiple Floor Patterns

You and your partner draw a diagram of your individual floor patterns. Practice each of these floor patterns separately one at a time. Then, perform each of the floor patterns at the same time in the same space. Conclude by describing the changing relationships that result from performing your respective floor patterns at the same time. You may need to have someone observe you and your partner as you move through the floor patterns to help you describe how you and your partner are relating to each other. You and your partner can also design other floor patterns to create new relationships.

Summary

Understanding how your movements affect other dancers or objects on the stage is critical to making a dance flow smoothly and with the correct intention. Practice moving within the space around objects alone and then with others as suggested in the improvisation activity that follows.

Challenges and Reflections

Begin this improvisation by creating a movement environment for yourself. You can do this by placing objects in the space. The objects you use should be large and stable so that you can move on them as well as move in a relationship to them. Now, position yourself at one side of the room with the goal of traveling around the room, finishing the exploration on the other side of the space. As you travel, stop by the various objects and continue to move in your personal space by exploring how you can move and relate to each object. Create as many relationships as possible with each object. Repeat this improvisation by using a different pathway or floor pattern as you move from object to object.

- Describe the movement relationships you created with each object you encountered. Did you move over, under, around, or in any other relationship to each object?
- Describe the floor pattern you used to move from one side of the room to the other side. Did this floor pattern contain straight or curved paths or a combination of these two possibilities?
- Describe how your body was supported throughout this improvisation.
- Did you create any short rhythmic patterns as you moved throughout the space? How can you describe the longer rhythmic pattern that resulted from your entire improvisation sequence?

chapter

5

Mastering the Principles of Movement

You've got the basics down—moving within your personal space and in relation to a partner. Now let's take it a step further. Six important movement principles affect every move you make: alignment, centering, gravity, balance, breathing, and tension and relaxation. Understanding these principles will help you refine your movements and give you a polished look that distinguishes a professional from a novice.

Alignment

Alignment is the placement of each segment of your body—the head, shoulders, torso, hips, and legs—in relation to one another. Usually we think of alignment while we are standing in one spot, but think about what happens to your alignment when you travel across space. When you stay in one spot and move in personal space, it is easier to keep your body aligned than when you move in general space. You can check your alignment from a side and a front view in the mirror.

Good alignment is the starting point for all dance movement; it is also important because misalignments can lead to physical stress and injuries. Thus, good alignment can improve your dancing by helping you move more efficiently. It can also lessen the chance of injuries and lengthen your performing life. Many people think of alignment as a static position of the body, but alignment is always movement oriented, or dynamic. When still, your body should be poised for action; when you are dancing, your alignment must respond to the constantly changing demands of moving in personal and general space. One way to think about alignment is to consider the relationship between different segments of the body—head, shoulders, torso, hips, and legs. The alignment of the body should be evaluated from three directions: side, front, and back of the body. From a profile view a straight line should pass just in front of the middle of the knee and ankle, and directly through the hip, shoulder, and lobe of the ear so that each of the body segments are stacked on top of one another (Howe & Oldham 1998).

CHECKING YOUR ALIGNMENT

Many common alignment problems are apparent when you look at the body from the side. It is easy to see whether your head is placed too far in front of or too far behind a vertical line. From the side, you can also see whether your shoulders round forward (known as *kyphosis*) or whether you have a swayed back (known as *lordosis*). Many people stand with their hips in a permanently bent position because they are not able to straighten this joint completely. Many tests can be used to evaluate your alignment from the side. One test is to hold a plumb bob (a string with a weight on the end of it) at the side of your body. You have good alignment if your ear, shoulder, hip, knee, and ankle are at or close to the string.

When you view your body from the side, you can also check to see whether your back is slightly curved or absolutely straight. A perfectly straight back is not natural or safe; the curves serve as shock absorbers when you stand or move.

Without these curves, your back is subjected to stress and possible injury. The curves of your back offset the weight of each body segment. Thus, the slightly forward position of your head is counterbalanced by the backward curve in your shoulders and upper back. It is easier to visualize the counterbalancing effect produced by the curves of your spine by thinking about the segments of your body as blocks. Your head is one block, your torso another, and so on. This means that the block represented by your head is slightly forward of the block representing your torso. Never try to stand so tall that you take the curves out of your back, because to do so will destroy the counterbalancing effect.

You can evaluate your alignment from the front of your body as well as from the side. From the front, your head should be straight, not tilted to one side or the other. The shoulders should be even, the hipbones should be even, and the knees should be even so that your shoulders, hips, and knees should fall on the same line parallel to the floor (see figure 5.1).

Good alignment also involves placing your weight on your feet so that it is evenly distributed between the inside and outside of the ball of each foot and evenly distributed between your toes and heels. You should not roll to the inside or outside of either foot or tip forward onto your toes or lean backward on your heels. If your weight is evenly distributed among the front, back, and sides of

FIGURE 5.1   Proper alignment.

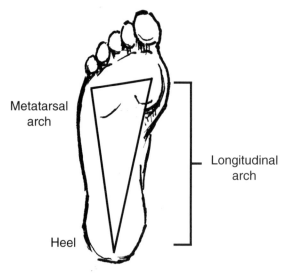

Metatarsal arch

Longitudinal arch

Heel

FIGURE 5.2   Triangle of weight.

each foot, it will fall into the shape of a triangle (see figure 5.2). Many dancers walk with their legs in turnout because this position is used in many dance movements. However, walking in turnout does throw your weight to the outside of your feet. To help distribute your weight evenly, walk with your toes directed straight ahead when you are not dancing. You can see how each of the alignment problems described can cause the segments of your body to move away from a straight line. Such deviations from good alignment are more common than you might think, because many people spend the better part of each day sitting in front of a computer or hunched over paperwork, causing their bodies to take on misaligned positions.

Barbara Plunk, at the University of California at Irvine dance program, developed a method of judging weight placement on the feet. In this test, the dancer stands on a box that has a glass top with a mirror located beneath the glass. The examiner uses this box, called a podiascope, to see whether dancers roll in or out on their feet or lean forward or backward; the mirror reflects weight placement of the feet on the glass. Foot problems not seen in a traditional visual exam are detected with a podiascope (Plastino 1990).

Good placement and movement habits also improve your alignment. When you begin to travel in general space, your alignment will naturally tilt into the direction of your movement. This tilt in your body helps you gain momentum for your movements. You may notice that runners in a track meet take advantage of this concept by beginning a race in a low, forward crouch. As you begin to travel, however, it is still important to keep your body segments aligned so that your whole body tilts into the direction of your movement. In some of the explorations you have already done, you practiced initiating movement by leading with your head or another part of your body. Leading into a movement with one part of your body, particularly with your head, begins to feel normal after a while. But do not begin all your movements in this way because it can destroy your body alignment.

IMPROVING YOUR ALIGNMENT

Body therapists help people rid themselves of bad movement habits. In fact, one of the bad habits that body therapists are concerned with is poor alignment. Moshe Feldenkrais, inventor of the *Feldenkrais Method* of body therapy, believed that people can correct misalignments of the body by becoming more aware of how they move. Another body therapist, Frederick Matthias Alexander, discovered that alignment could be improved through correct placement of the head. Alexander called poor placement of the head and other bad habits "misuse of the body" (Knaster 1996).

One of the most effective methods for improving your alignment is to have a balanced body. This means that the muscles on one side of your body should be as equal as possible in strength and elasticity to the muscles on the other side of the body. For example, if you have shoulders that round forward, then the muscles at the front of your shoulders are excessively strong and tight, and the muscles at the back of your shoulders are weak and excessively elastic. If you stand with a swayed back, the muscles at the front of your torso are weak and overly elastic, whereas the muscles at the small of your back are too strong and tight.

Dancing requires frequent use of second position, in which the arms are held out to the side of the body. This position can strain the muscles of the upper back and make your shoulders extremely tense. You can reduce stress in your shoulders by strengthening the muscles of your upper back and by learning to reach outward, away from the center of your body, when your arms are in second position. Avoid pinching your shoulder blades together because this will increase tension in your shoulders and affect the alignment of your body (see figure 5.3).

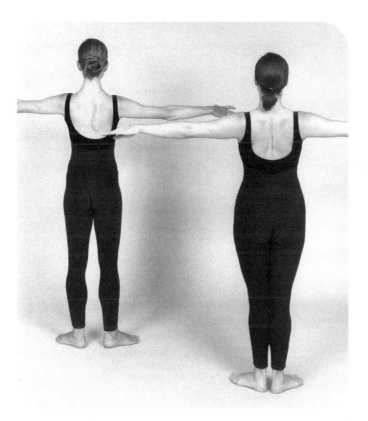

FIGURE 5.3   Pinching the shoulder blades together (right) increases tension in the upper body.

The lower part of the back can present problems as well. Many dance movements occur with the legs turned out at the hips. If you do not have much natural turnout, however, you may find that you must overarch your back to increase your turnout. This use of the back, or lordosis, is usually accompanied by pushing the ribs too far forward. Lordosis is also connected to pushing the knees backward so that they become overly straight *(hyperextended)*. Fifth is an example of a dance position in which a beginning dancer might be tempted to distort the alignment of the body to achieve outward rotation. Also avoid rotating at the knees because the knees, as you will remember from chapter 2, are only meant to bend and straighten. When you stand with your toes straight ahead, and twist your body around to the side, resist twisting your knees to get into this or other similar positions (see figure 5.4).

Finally, we come to the way you use your feet. Excessive turnout can cause you to roll inward on your arches, a position known as *pronation*. In particular, pronation with excessive turnout can be a problem when you rise to three-quarter point; this position can cause the weight to shift inward (see figure 5.5). In three-quarter point in turnout, keep your weight centered on the ball of your foot. Good alignment is a must because problems with alignment at one place in your body will set off a chain reaction and cause alignment problems in other parts of your body.

FIGURE 5.4   Twisting at the knees (left) is dangerous.

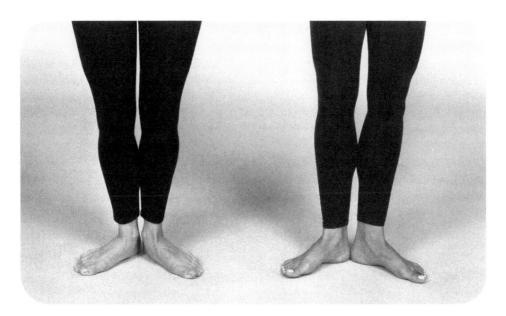

FIGURE 5.5   The dancer on the left is rolling in on the arches (pronating).

Alignment Self-Check

Stand in profile in front of a mirror. In this position, your feet are slightly apart with your toes pointing straight ahead. Then, begin at the top of your body and check to see whether your ear, shoulder, and hip fall on a vertical line that meets the floor at a right angle. This same line, known as the *line of gravity*, should also go slightly in front of the middle of your knee and slightly in front of your ankle. You might also like to have someone else check your alignment by holding a weighted string next to the side of your body. This string should be in line with your ear, shoulder, and hip. Now, move your body so that your ear, shoulder, hip, knee, and ankle are no longer in line. To do this you can poke you head forward, push your hips forward or backward, or tilt your whole body backward from your hips. Try some of these variations and focus on how it feels to be misaligned.

Next, turn your body so that you are facing the mirror. Again, your feet should be slightly apart with the toes pointing straight ahead. Make sure your head is straight, not tilted to one side or the other. Your shoulders, hips, and knees should also be at the same level from the floor. Finally, examine your feet from the front of your body. If your weight is placed solidly on your feet, both the inner and outer edges of each foot will be flat on the floor, and you will not roll in on your arches or onto the outside of your feet. You can also check the weight placement on your feet by looking at the wear patterns on the soles of your shoes. If the soles of your shoes are more worn at the outside, you carry your weight at the outside of your feet, or *supinate*. More wear on the inside means that you roll in on your arches, or pronate. If you lean forward or backward, the worn area on your shoes would be at the front or back of the soles. Try some variations on frontal alignment by raising one shoulder, dropping your weight into one hip, or standing with more weight on one foot.

Alignment in General Space

When you begin to move, your alignment will naturally tilt in the direction of your movement, but the segments of your body should still be in a straight line. Begin to walk forward so that you are moving throughout the general space of the room. As you walk, watch your body in profile in the mirror. You should be able to see that the alignment of your body tilts slightly forward in the direction of your movement. You should also be able to feel this slight forward tilt. Now, continue to walk, but distort your alignment by throwing a part of your body out in front or behind the line of gravity. You should find that it is more difficult to move throughout space when your body is misaligned.

Relating Alignment, Direction, and Speed

Begin by walking throughout general space. This time, gradually increase the speed of your walking until you are moving so rapidly that you have to run. When you run, you should feel your alignment tilt even farther forward than when you were walking. Now, slow down to a walk. You should again feel a change in your body as your alignment moves closer to the vertical. Finally, continue to walk in general space, but change both the direction and tempo of your movements. Go forward, backward, sideways, and diagonally as you change the speed of your movements at the same time. As you move, look at your alignment in the mirror. You should notice that your whole body tilts slightly into each new direction. You should also be able to feel the changes in the tilt of your body as you begin to travel in each new direction.

Centering

Centering relates to the location of the physical center (center of gravity) of your body and to a way of moving, but it also refers to a psychological feeling of connectedness between the mind and the body and of being secure. Physical center is more concrete, whereas psychological center is a concept of mind.

PHYSICAL CENTER

Your physical center of gravity is located in the pelvis, slightly below the navel. It is the most dense part of your body. From profile view in a standing position, the line of alignment passes through your center of gravity, through your base of support, and connects with the center of the earth. Your sense of center of gravity is important because you must be able to control and manipulate your center of gravity in dance class and performance. Earlier in this chapter you learned that in good alignment, the segments of your body are stacked one on top of the other. Thus, if you want to stay in one place, you will need to keep your center of gravity over your base. You can also resist moving by reaching another part of your body out from your center in a direction opposite to the direction of your movement. Moving, however, means disturbing your stability and taking your center of gravity beyond your base of support. Moving also involves lifting your center as a preparation for movement. So if you want to move forward quickly, you must have your weight lifted and poised slightly forward ready for action. You are not ready if your weight is back on your heels. (See figure 5.6.)

You also change the location of your center of gravity when you add a weight to your moving body. If you stand with a book in your outstretched hand, your body's center of gravity will shift in the direction of your outstretched hand holding the book. Lifts have the same effect on the location of the center of gravity: The placement of the second dancer affects the location of the center of gravity of the first dancer. In other words, the dancers' combined center of gravity shifts into the direction of the added body weight unless the second dancer is directly above the supporting dancer. Thus, to continue dancing without excess stress, the partners must position their bodies so that their center of gravity is over or almost over their base of support (see figure 5.7).

Body structure is a final factor that affects the location of physical center. In this respect, the center of gravity is usually located lower in the body for women than for men, because most women's hips are wider than men's. A short person will also have a lower center of gravity than a tall person. Young children have a higher center of gravity, however, because they have a relatively large, heavy head in comparison to the size and weight of their bodies. For this reason, young children can be very unstable. Location of the center of gravity also varies for the three body types *ectomorph*, *mesomorph* and *endomorph*. According to this theory,

FIGURE 5.6   Dancer on left is poised for movement.

FIGURE 5.7   The lift performed by the dancers on the right is easier to do.

ectomorphs have long, lean, narrow bodies with rather fragile bones, and their hips are wider than their shoulders. In contrast, mesomorphs are short and much more muscular. Their shoulders are wide and their hips are narrow. The structure of the typical endomorph falls somewhere between that of an ectomorph and a mesomorph. Thus, a body that combines the characteristics of the mesomorph and endomorph has the greatest mass and a lowest center of gravity. People with such a body type make excellent football linemen, but they are not built as typical dancers (see figure 5.8). The exact location of the center of gravity can be calculated mathematically through a technique known as *underwater weighing*.

Kinesiologists (those who study human movement) identify one center in the body, but others acknowledge three separate center zones (Blair 2002a). The shoulder zone is the area from the top of the shoulders down to the bottom of the rib cage. The center zone goes from the lower edge of the ribs to the upper edge of the hips. The hip zone extends from the top of the hipbone to the point at which the leg connects to the hip. The overall center zone ties all three zones together. By placing a support belt around your waist, you can pull all three zones together. You should place this belt so that its top barely covers the lower ribs and the bottom just touches the upper part of the hipbones. You can also get your center zones under control by pulling all your abdominal muscles up into the

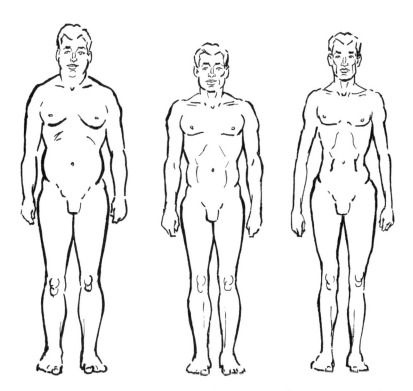

FIGURE 5.8 Three body types: endomorph, mesomorph, and ectomorph.

center of your body. Once you have control of your center, you can locate your center point of balance. The center point of balance is located in the same place for everyone: in the center of the body where the two sides of the rib cage come together. This means that the center point of balance is above your waist and above your navel as well. So the location of your center point of balance and your center of gravity are not the same. By initiating movement from your center point of balance, however, you can experience a feeling of cooperation in all three zones. By moving in this way, you feel secure and as though you have control over your movements. The center point of balance is also known as the solar plexus.

PSYCHOLOGICAL CENTER

A dancer who uses the center effectively will move differently than one who does not grasp this concept. Alma Hawkins, creator of the dance program at UCLA, describes the centered dancer as being able to move from within and use the center as a source for each action. The psychological center is an idea that does not necessarily refer to the physical center of the body, but to a source of energy and feeling for dancing. If a dancer is centered, movements seem to flow from the torso. In turn, the dancer's arms and legs appear connected to the center of the body. The center is the source of movement vitality. The centered dancer appears to be absorbed in the act of dancing and has the ability to connect with observers and project to the audience (Hawkins 1988).

FIGURE 5.9   Example of African dance pose.

An understanding of psychological center can give you an advantage. You may feel stronger when your moves are aligned and solid. Psychological center also involves bringing your mental focus to your center so that your mind and body come together. It is a feeling of moving your body as a whole rather than part by part. When you are centered you are able to gather energy from the earth and let it flow through your body. To experience this feeling, think of standing with your knees bent and your feet flat on the floor. Then, see energy streaming upward from the earth through your legs and into the center of your body (Lidell 1987).

The idea of center and connecting with the earth is a common element in African dance. For example, stamping is a traditional African dance element; it represents the union of human and earth. The Zulu believe echoes from the earth are symbols of growth. To emphasize the connection with the earth, Zulu dancers squat and shuffle their feet to embrace the ground and draw power from it (see figure 5.9). African dancers want to connect with the earth because they regard it as friendly rather than an environment that they must escape (Asante 1996). In contrast, many Western forms of dance seek to escape the pull of the earth.

Using Center As an Energy Source

Stand in one spot with your heels together and your arms at your sides. You may recognize this placement of the feet as first position. Now, begin to sway in a sustained manner so that your whole body goes from side to side as you shift your weight first to one foot and then to the other. Next, stop swaying and then begin again, but this time focus on the center of your body. Try to initiate the swaying action from your center by moving the center of your body first before you move the other parts of your body. The feeling you experience in your body should be one of pulling in opposite directions between your center and your feet, the base. Next, extend this exploration by holding a book or other fairly heavy object out to the side of your body as you sway. Continue, however, to let your other arm rest at your side. You should find that you must consciously pull your body back in the opposite direction from the hand holding the object. You might like to try swaying in other directions to see what effect this has on your ability to remain centered. Put the object down, and challenge yourself by swaying as far as you can from side to side before you fall off center.

Isadora Duncan *on body center as soul*

The use of the center of your body as the energy center or as psychological center is not an entirely new idea in Western dance. Isadora Duncan, often called the mother of modern dance, expressed herself without using existing dance forms. She frequently talked about the center of the body and called it the soul. In the Duncan style, the torso is trained so that the legs' movements flowed throughout the whole body rather than being cut off at the hips. Duncan also believed that the body's center should be used to lead movement. Thus, when Duncan danced, she often looked like the figurehead on a ship with the torso leaning forward and the limbs trailing behind (see figure 5.10). Duncan believed that the body should move first in locomotor actions with the arms following in an unfolding action from the upper arms through the lower arms and fingers. When movements flowed through the body in this way, they looked graceful and satisfying (Blair 1986). In a Duncan leap, movement also traveled from the center, but it moved more slowly through the arms and back leg. This use of movement gave the dancer the illusion of weightlessness. The lightweight draperies that Duncan and her troupe wore—including a flowing, Grecian tunic or dress that was her favorite costume—also added to the impression of lightness.

FIGURE 5.10   Isadora Duncan.

Reprinted, by permission, from Jerome Robbins Dance Division, The New York Public Library for the Performing Arts: Ascot, Lenor, and Tilden Foundations.

Doris Humphrey *on gut feeling*

Doris Humphrey (1987), an American modern dance pioneer and talented teacher, believed that deeply felt emotions begin in the middle of the body where the vital organs are located. She added that in real life, the first part of an emotional response is in the center of the body; then the hands reach to the head or to the upper part of the body. Of course, Humphrey did not mean that the movements that accompany these emotions were the materials of a dance. Instead, she believed that this connection between movement and feeling was the starting point for movement discovery and dance making (see figure 5.11).

FIGURE 5.11   Doris Humphrey.

Doris Humphrey in *To The Dance*. Photo by Bois, collection of Charles H. Woodford.

Using Your Center While Traveling

This exploration is designed to help you use your center to encourage moving across space. Begin this exploration by walking forward throughout the space. Initiate your walking, however, by lifting and pressing the center of your body forward into the direction in which you are moving. At the same time, move in a sustained manner, and keep your body aligned. As you continue to move, imagine that someone is pulling on a string attached to the center of your body. The feeling should be one of strength and of initiating movement from your center. Now, continue to walk throughout the room, but let your center drop toward the floor. If you perform this action correctly, it should look as though you are sinking into each hip as you walk. It should also feel as if you are dropping your weight into each hip as you take each step. Compare the two ways of walking that you explored. How did the center of your body feel when you walked in the first way? What about when you walked in the second way?

Finding the Energy Center

Stand in one spot with your feet placed under your shoulders. Then, reach slowly to one side, but start this action in the center of your body. If you do this action correctly, the movement will gradually travel outward from your center to your arm. To help you perform this action, focus on the image and feeling of energy flowing from your center out to your fingertips. Repeat this same exploration using light and heavy energy qualities and free and bound flow as well. You should find that it is easier to feel the energy flowing from your center when you use a heavy energy quality and also during bound flow.

Gravity

Whether you are standing still or moving, you must relate to the pull of gravity. Sometimes gravity helps you do a movement, and at other times it slows your actions to a standstill. As long as you remain on earth you will have to relate to the pull of gravity. Gravity acts on all matter and pulls everything toward the center of the planet, forming a bond with the earth. Among living things, however, there is a tendency to act against gravity. This second force is antigravity. Thus, when you grow or move upward, you are counteracting the pull of gravity to cause a constant interplay between these two forces. Many of the forms and designs found in nature have a spiral shape that reflects the interplay between the upward and downward forces. Such spiral shapes are found in tornadoes and in water going down a drain. The human body also contains many spiral shapes in bones and muscles and the movement of various fluids.

Common movements and complex dance actions are all affected by gravity; the only way to escape gravity is to travel to outer space. But even though we try to escape gravity, our very survival depends on it. In fact, our experiences with space travel have shown that zero gravity affects our health, causing our bones to thin.

The efforts of babies to stand and walk also represent the interaction of gravity and antigravity. The first attempts babies make to travel across space involve wriggling and rocking actions. Later, these simple movements develop into a reaching of the baby's head forward and pulling the tailbone backward to prepare the arms and legs to support the body. As babies move into each stage of development on the way to standing, they go through a specific sequence of reaching and pulling patterns. Each of these movement sequences must be mastered or the baby will feel lost or ungrounded.

The physical effect of gravity on the human body is described in terms of the center of gravity and the line of gravity. Gravity operates while you are both standing and moving. As soon as the force that causes movement is spent, however, gravity takes over and the movement comes to a rest. In some types of movement it is natural to resist gravity, and in other actions gravity helps propel movements. When you get up out of a chair or lift your leg, you must resist the pull of gravity. But when you swing your arms, gravity initiates the downward part of the swing. Thus, you must pull away from gravity on the upward part of a swing and give into gravity on the downward part of this action. Gravity also assists locomotor movements: As you shift your center of gravity beyond your base of support, you begin to fall, and your innate response is to walk or run to stay on your feet. The position in which you put your whole body or a part of your body is affected by gravity as well. It is more difficult to hold a straight leg out in front of your body than it is to hold a bent leg in the same position. When your leg is straight, gravity pulls down on all segments of your leg. In the bent position, gravity pulls down on the thigh segment only, and it seems as though your leg is shorter and weighs less.

Human beings are either in motion, poised for action, or at rest. While you are moving you must constantly adjust to the pull of gravity—a process that is automatic once it is learned. Doris Humphrey created much of her dance technique around the gravity principle and its effect on the body, because she felt that giving in to gravity and rebounding from it were at the core of human movement. Humphrey claimed that all dancing went back and forth between two points: the vertical and the horizontal, or life and death. She called the experience of dancing between these two points *fall and recovery*. In the Humphrey technique, falling starts from a static point of equilibrium. Falling is slow at first, and then it accelerates as gravity takes over. When it seems as though the dancer is about to collapse, however, a rebound occurs and the body springs back to life—unless the dancer wants to fall to the ground. After the rebound, there is a momentary suspension and return to equilibrium so that the process can start over (Stodell 1978).

Relating to Gravity in Personal Space

Stand in one spot with your feet under your shoulders. Then, lift one arm high to the side of your body. Next, let your arm drop (give into gravity) so that it swings from side to side. You should find that the pull of gravity gradually slows the swinging of your arm so that it comes to rest at your side. Now, lift your arm up to the side one more time, and let it go again to repeat the swing. As you do this, watch your swinging arm in the mirror to make sure that it travels through an arc in space as it goes from side to side. You should also feel the heaviness in your arm as you let it give in to gravity and the pulling sensation as you lift your arm away from gravity at the beginning of each swinging action. Challenge yourself by performing the same arm swing, beginning the movement from different directions and different levels.

Relating to Gravity in General Space

Stand with your heels together (first position) and your arms at your sides. Then, start to sway from side to side. This time you are going to sway so much that you give in to the pull of gravity by falling. Do not fall, however, but resist the pull of gravity by taking several steps to bring your body back to its original, upright position. Repeat this exploration by swaying and falling in other directions. When you watch this exploration in a mirror, you should see your center move out beyond your base. You should also see the path you follow as you attempt to regain the centered position. The feelings you experience in your body should be swaying, falling, traveling through space, and becoming centered again.

Relating Gravity to Body Shape

Stand in one spot with your feet beneath your shoulders. You might also like to place one hand on the wall or other stable object. You will put your right leg into three positions: First, lift your leg directly in front of your body with the knee straight. Next, lift your leg forward again, but bend your knee slightly. Finally, lift the same leg in front of your body a third time, but bend your knee as much as you can. Check each of these three actions in a mirror to make sure that your knee is straight, bent slightly, and then bent as much as possible. You should find that the first leg lift feels heavier than the other two because gravity is pulling down on all segments of your leg. Try swinging your leg while it is bent and also while it is straight. Does it seem easier to swing your leg while it is bent? (See figure 5.12.)

FIGURE 5.12   Relating the pull of gravity to body shape.

Balance

Balance is a body feeling of being poised or in a state of equilibrium. If you are balanced, you are centered and will not fall by giving in to the pull of gravity. Balance is exciting when you achieve it but frustrating when you lose it. As a student of dance, surely you have encountered some problems with balance. Skill in balancing is, of course, intimately connected to your alignment, use of center, and relationship to gravity. Your ability to balance also depends on your body awareness.

Balancing while you are motionless *(static balance)* is easier than trying to balance while you are moving *(dynamic balance)*. Static balance requires no extra effort to control for the effects of movement on the alignment of your body. You can use retraining methods for each type of balance. To retrain static balance, use rigid supports such as wall bars. Then, as balance improves, remove the supports. To improve dynamic balance, increase the support, but these supports must be moveable. You can use large, inflatable fitness balls and wobble boards to provide the added support. (A wobble board is a half-sphere attached to a board on which you stand. Balance is improved by keeping the middle of the sphere in contact with the floor.)

Three factors determine your ability to balance. The first of these factors is the size of your base of support. Balance is usually not a problem when you are lying down or seated because the base of support is quite large. You can also easily maintain balance by standing with your feet apart. In contrast, your base of support while standing on one foot is much smaller, presenting a more challenging balance problem. The ultimate challenge is dancing on point because the base of support is so small (see figure 5.13). The second factor in balancing is the height of your center of gravity from the ground. Thus, it is more difficult to balance with a high rather than a low center of gravity. Short dancers are able to balance more easily than their tall counterparts.

The third factor that affects balance involves both the base of support and center of gravity. To balance, you must keep your center over your base so that the line of gravity falls through the base. This requirement is fairly simple to maintain in some dance forms but not in others. For example, tap and classical ballet dancers usually have their center over their base, but in modern or jazz dance the body is frequently shifted off center (see figure 5.14).

FIGURE 5.13   Small base of support on point.

FIGURE 5.14 The dancer on the right is shifting her center beyond her base of support.

Dancers are not satisfied for long doing actions in the vertical plane because they soon discover reasons for moving that cause them to do irregular and precarious movements in which the arms and upper body reach to one side or the hips are thrust to the front or back. The side tilt in modern dance is an example of such an off-center position. In *balance and compensation*, when a body part or parts move away from the line of gravity, another part of the body must be moved in the opposite direction to stabilize the body (Hawkins 1988). For example, you can balance more easily in the tilt if you counterbalance the high side reach of your upper body by stretching your lifted leg low to the opposite side. You will also improve your balance in this position if you let your energy flow out from your center through your arms and legs in opposite directions (see figure 5.15).

Balancing during movement presents other challenges because you need to balance on a constantly shifting base. The tempo at which you move is also a factor in the balancing equation. You should use a gradual approach to learn to balance while moving: Walk with small steps in the beginning, and slowly lengthen your stride. Then increase the tempo so that your walk gradually turns into a run. Combining walking and running in a single movement sequence can also make you aware of the greater lean of the body in a run. Running flatfooted disturbs balance, so pay attention to the rolling action of your feet. Add arm movements only after you have mastered balance while traveling without moving the arms.

FIGURE 5.15 A tilt uses balance and compensation.

You can use a technique called three-toe base to improve balance. This technique, developed by Skippy Blair, involves the area between the base of the first three toes and the ends of the same toes. In this technique, you focus on pressing the first three toes against the floor to move the body forward. If you use the three-toe base, you need to pretend that your little toe and the one next to it do not exist. This approach to locomotion helps dancers feel balanced and in control. When dancers use their feet in this way, they also look more lifted in the center of the body.

You have learned that in good alignment the muscles on opposite sides of the body should be equal or nearly equal in strength and elasticity. A lack of strength can affect balance as well, especially when you attempt to balance on three-quarter point or on point. If the muscles on the inside of your ankle are weak, you will roll inward in relevé. If the muscles at the outside of your ankle are weak, the opposite balance problem will occur—you will roll to the outside of your foot in relevé.

Skill in balancing is tied to the less concrete concept of body awareness and the psychological aspects of center. Remember that body awareness involves having an accurate sense of where you are moving in space and what parts of your body are moving. Body awareness also involves knowing how movements are performed and recognizing the relationship between your body and objects and with other dancers. Thus, increased body awareness will help you balance; you will sense what you need to do to maintain your equilibrium. Having the psychological sensation of alignment and poise in your body will make it easier for you to balance.

Tai chi chuan involves balance because it is based on the principles of yin and yang, or soft and hard forces. The postures in tai chi are performed with awareness, calmness, clarity, and equilibrium so that the mover can shift seamlessly from one posture to the next. You move in perfect balance in tai chi, so there is no strain and you are grounded, aligned, and aware (Knaster 1996). Balance is a frustrating thing. You may think you have it conquered, only to find that it has slipped from your grasp. Such variations occur because the connection between your mind and body changes from day to day. One day you may feel confident and together, and at another time you may be more scattered. If you are tired, your balance can also be off.

Balancing on Different Supports

Stand with your feet apart under your shoulders; lift your arms out to the side of your body. Then, tilt your whole body to your right so that you are balanced on one foot. Complete the balance on one foot by pressing up to a half-point position. Next, return to the stance in which your feet are under your shoulders, and do the same tilt to the left side. You will end in a tilt to the left while you balance on half point on one foot. Check each of these positions in a mirror to make sure that your body is straight and then tilted and that you are standing first on two feet and then on one foot. Compare your ability to balance in the different positions. You will probably experience the most difficulty while trying to balance on half point because your base of support is so small.

Balancing at Different Levels

Position your feet under your shoulders with your arms out at the sides of your body. Then, bend your knees. Next, straighten your knees, and press up to half point. Check each of these positions in the mirror. Make sure that you move from a position in which your knees are bent to one in which your knees are straight, and finally to a position in which you are balanced on half point. Move through the same three positions again, but concentrate on how each one feels in your body. The balance on half point should feel less stable than the other two positions, because your base of support is so small and the center of your body is higher as well. Challenge yourself by balancing at three different levels using an asymmetrical body shape. You can also test your balance in general space by walking at the three different levels. Thus, you would walk with your knees bent, with your knees straight, and also while on half point.

Balance and Compensation

Assume a position in which you balance on one foot while your body is parallel to the floor. Your arms will be extended above your head and your free leg will reach directly behind your body. To help you balance in this position, reach out from your center through your arms and free leg. As you reach, you should feel energy traveling out from your center to the front and back in opposite directions. This opposing use of energy is an example of balance and compensation as described in the preceding section of this chapter. To complete this exploration, assume the same balanced position on one foot. This time, however, let your arms and leg droop or relax. You should find that it is much easier to balance when you are reaching out from your center in opposite directions than when your body is relaxed. (See figure 5.16.)

FIGURE 5.16   Balancing on one foot while arms are parallel to the floor is an example of balance and compensation.

Breathing

When you breathe with your movements, your actions have a feeling of vitality. Movement that is not energized will not project to the audience. In general, dancers breathe in to lift or suspend movement, and they breathe out when they give in to the pull of gravity. This method of breathing encourages the flow of energy from the center of the body and contributes to body awareness. Moving with awareness and vitality also means filling different parts of the body with breath. Nondancers may think that the idea of breathing into a part of the body is unusual, but trained dancers do this all the time. Dancers can breathe with the whole body or into many body parts. In fact, breathing into different parts of the body appears natural and satisfying to the observer.

Breathing techniques have long been used in many forms of exercise and body work to encourage alertness and relaxation. Breathing can also be used to release energy at points in the body where it is blocked. Breath work is an integral part of yoga; it is used to slow breathing, expand lung capacity, and build energy. Breathing is also an important part of the body therapy system called *Bartenieff Fundamentals.* The Bartenieff technique breathing allows a person to feel the connection among the different body parts and between the whole body and the surroundings. Breath should be experienced as a centering activity so that it enlarges support to and from the core of the body. Breathing also helps dancers connect with the audience and enhance expression because it energizes the body.

Breathing in Personal Space

Find a position in which your body is low and close to the floor. Then, inhale using your breath to lift your body away from the floor. End your upward movement by reaching as high as you can. Slowly descend back to the floor and exhale as you go down. You should be able to see your mirror image grow larger as you rise and become smaller as you collapse back to the floor. As you inhale, your body will feel like a large balloon that is being inflated; as you exhale and move to the floor, you will feel as though you have let the air out of the balloon. You might also like to try inhaling and exhaling into a single part of your body. Here, inhaling would cause you to reach the body part out into your personal space, whereas exhaling causes a collapse of this part of the body.

Breathing in General Space

Select several locomotor movements, but make sure that these movements change level. For example, a leap begins at low level and goes to high level, ending with a landing on a bent leg at a lower level. Practice each of the locomotor movements you have selected. Perform these same actions again, but this time inhale as you go up and exhale as you descend. You should find that breathing in this way makes each of these locomotor moves easier to perform. The upward part of the locomotor moves should also feel lighter when you emphasize your breathing in this way.

Breath-Motivated Movements

Inhale slowly, and let the inhalation of each breath move you across space. You will continue to travel in the same direction until you can no longer inhale. Then, let your breath out and go in a new direction. Continue breathing in and out going in a new direction with each inhalation and exhalation. You should discover that by breathing in this way your movements develop into short sequences, or pieces, of movement. You should also be able to see the beginning and ending of each movement sequence in a mirror and feel each beginning and ending movement in your body.

Tension and Relaxation

Tension is a state of contraction in your muscles. It is important to use varying degrees of tension and relaxation in your muscles so that you can perform movements in various ways. Many people go through life holding excessive tension in their bodies. Usually they do not realize that they are carrying around this tension until they relax and experience the difference between a tense state and a relaxed state.

People acquire bad movement habits through poor posture or improper body mechanics. Such bad habits create excess tension in the body. People retain such patterns through habit because they begin to feel comfortable after a time. You can get a better handle on your tension patterns by becoming more aware of how tension can build up in your body. As you go about your daily routine, scan your body for such tension patterns.

The signs of stress or tension that are easiest to spot are frequent illness, constant occurrence of injuries, and overall fatigue. Emotional displays that are out of character, oversensitivity, moodiness, and depression can also point to stress. The way dancers talk about themselves can point to stress as well. Students who feel negative about themselves or their performance or lack self-confidence usually experience more stress (Taylor & Taylor 1995). Finally, dancers with declining performance abilities or who no longer are motivated to dance could also be under a great deal of stress.

Exercise is recommended for relieving tension because it can get your mind off of your problems. Most dancers get plenty of exercise, yet they still have problems with stress. Thus, the key is to find a strategy for dealing with situations that cause tension. This may mean coming early to class so that you do not feel rushed, using relaxation techniques before a performance, or taking time to wind down and stretch out after dancing. You might also like to do relaxation exercises at the end of each day.

If you are under stress, try to change situations that cause stress. This may mean talking to a counselor or having a discussion with your teachers and parents—all of whom may be able to help you discover new ways to deal with problematic situations. Constantly focusing on the end product or performance can be very stressful too. Instead, emphasize the process of preparing for a performance rather than just concentrating on the outcome. Take some time off if you

feel tired so that you do not overtrain. Sign up for a lighter class load or partici-
pate in other activities for a summer. It can also be helpful to approach dancing
with an attitude of having fun so that you think about your time dancing as
something other than serious work.

There are also some practical, short-term methods for dealing with stress. The
first of these techniques, controlled breathing, involves taking deep, rhythmic
breaths to replenish your oxygen supply. When you are under stress, your breathing becomes short and choppy, cutting off your supply of oxygen. Deep breathing also takes your focus off negative feelings you may have. Progressive relaxation is also a practical technique. In this method, you contract the muscles you
want to relax. Then, you let go of the tension and take a deep breath. Progressive
relaxation makes you aware of how tension feels in your muscles. Your muscles
rebound in response to the heightened tension produced by the contraction, and
they go to a more relaxed state. Another short-term remedy for stress is to smile.
You will probably find that when you smile while you dance, your bodily tension
will seem to disappear (Taylor & Taylor 1995).

The constructive rest position, developed by kinesiologist Lulu Sweigard, is
another short-term method for reducing stress. To assume this position, lie on
the floor and bend your knees approximately 90 degrees so that your feet are flat
on the floor close to your hips. Position your feet so that they are in line with
your hips and your toes are pointing straight ahead. To complete the constructive
rest position, fold your arms across the front of your chest. Do not grip your body
with your hands, however. If you have trouble maintaining the foot and leg position, tie your thighs together just above the knees (see figure 5.17). You may wish
to place a small pillow under your head (not your neck) to maintain the alignment of your head and upper body. Constructive rest is relaxing because it is a
position that requires little or no muscular effort. Constructive rest also uses gravity
to reduce muscle strain and produce a balanced relaxation of the muscles in the
whole body.

FIGURE 5.17   Constructive rest position.

Knaster (1996) used the word *tensegrity* to describe the relationship between relaxation and tension. When our muscles are balanced, the body is aligned. Balance becomes disturbed, however, if the muscles get too tight. Thus, if this problem occurs, the bones under your muscles have to lean in one direction or another to accommodate the lack of balance, and the tensegrity (or relationship between the bones and muscles) is disturbed. In any case, you must learn to deal with tension for two reasons. First, habitual tension patterns interfere with coordination and block the flow of energy in your body—an outcome that decreases your body awareness and movement vitality. Second, habitual tension patterns can put strain on parts of your body and eventually lead to injury.

As you can see, the ability to relax is influenced by many factors. Relaxation is difficult for many people because the doing part of the nervous system pulls people back to activity. Such people find that being at rest causes anxiety and a fear of being stuck. People who are outwardly focused need time to relax and look inward, whereas those who are more receptive to their inner state should be encouraged to focus outward. In this way, a balance can be achieved between these two states.

Tension and Relaxation in Personal Space

Lie down on the floor and take several deep breaths to release the tension from your body. Focus on your right arm and make the muscles in this arm as tight as you can. Next, release the tension from your arm and take a deep breath. Now, try to remember the body feeling that you experienced when your arm was tense and when it was relaxed. Compare these two feelings. You should notice that there is a hard, compressed feeling in your arm when you tighten your muscles, and there is a soft feeling when the muscles are relaxed. Try tensing and relaxing other parts of your body then tensing and relaxing your whole body. Again, compare the body feelings you experienced in each of these exercises.

Tension and Relaxation in General Space

Walk throughout the room, but do so using light and then heavy energy qualities. Continue to walk, but change your use of energy to free and then bound flow. You should find that a light use of energy and free flow feel relatively relaxed, whereas heavy energy and bound flow are more tight. Continue to walk using the same four types of energy. Then, draw as many comparisons as you can between the four uses of energy by describing the different body feelings you experience.

Tension and Energy Flow

Walk throughout the room, but this time swing your arms as much as you can. As you walk and swing your arms, you should feel energy flowing from the center of your body out to your hands. Now, tense your body as much as you can, and continue to walk and swing your arms. Then, compare the two styles of walking. In the first walk, you should be able to feel energy flowing freely from your center into your arms. In the second version of the walk, however, you may have noticed that your energy did not flow as easily. In fact, in the second version of the walk, the flow of your energy may have felt as though it was blocked at some point or points between your center and your hands.

Summary

By evaluating your alignment and center of gravity as well as concepts such as balance, breathing, and tension and relaxation, you will have the knowledge to take your dance techniques to the next level. Practice incorporating these ideas in the improvisation activity that follows.

Challenges and Reflections

Select two nonlocomotor actions and two locomotor actions. Then, move through-out the room using only these four actions. Repeat each movement as many times as you like, and perform the four actions in any order.

- Describe the alignment of your body as you performed both the nonlocomotor and locomotor movements. Were the segments of your body in line or out of line as you did these movements? And did the alignment of your body seem to tilt in a particular direction, or was it straight up and down in relation to the floor?
- Next, talk about your use of center. When was your center over your base, and when was it not? Do you think that your energy flowed from the center of your body throughout the improvisation?
- During this improvisation you probably gave in to gravity at times and pulled away from it at other times. When did you give in to gravity, and when did you pull away from it?
- Describe the size of your base of support and the height of your center at different points during the improvisation.
- Did you use balance and compensation at any point in this improvisation?
- Do you think that your use of breath helped in your performance of the improvisation? If your breath helped you do these movements, explain why.
- Where in this improvisation did you feel tense? At what points were you relaxed?

chapter

6

Expressing Form

You've got the fundamentals down. Now it's time to have some fun and get creative! Use what you've learned in chapters 1 through 5 and expand your mind into creating movements that have meaning and which send a message. The emphasis of this chapter is on how movements look, the way they are combined, and how they communicate.

In this chapter you will explore body lines, planes of movement, and group shapes. You are also going to look at how to use pathways in more advanced ways, make bridges (transitions) between movement sequences, and order and pattern your movements. You may be surprised to discover that body line can mean several things: It can be the lines created in space by the shape of a dancer's body or by the shape of body parts. An observer can also create body lines by visually tracing a line from one point on a dancer's body to another. In addition, when a body line is moved in space, it creates a flat, two-dimensional shape called a *plane*. In chapter 2 you worked with body shape as it relates to a single dancer. In this chapter you will explore group shape, or shapes that are created by relationships between two or more dancers. The order you select for a series of movements is important as well. For example, if you create a series of actions that goes from high to low to middle level, it will have a different effect on the audience than a movement series that goes from middle to low to high level. So a different order creates a different relationship between the individual movements. Finally, the relationship between single movements and between movement sequences is described in this chapter as a *pattern*.

Body Line

Dance critics frequently talk about a performance by describing the lines of a single dancer's body or the lines created in space by several dancers' bodies. The question, however, is what does the term *line* mean? At the most concrete level, it is the visible line formed by a dancer's body or by parts of a dancer's body. When you stand with the segments of your body one above the other in good alignment, your body makes a straight shape that follows a straight line from head to toe. From this position, you can bend your knees and curve your body so that it forms the letter C. Now you are making a curved line with your body instead of a straight line. You can also make curved and straight lines with a single part of your body. If you lift one arm to the side, you can do so in two ways. You can lift your arm so that it forms a straight line from the fingers to the shoulder. You can also bend your elbow slightly so that you are making a curved line with your arm (see figure 6.1). Figure 6.2 shows a dancer in *arabesque* position. As you look at this figure, you should see that the dancer is making several straight lines in space with different parts of her body. In fact, her arms and legs radiate from her center in straight lines that are like the spokes on a bicycle wheel. A vertical line is created when a dancer stands upright. And a simple way to make a horizontal line with your body is to lie down on the floor. You can also create oblique, or slanted, body lines. These body lines are created when a dancer tilts the body at other than a 90-degree angle in relation to the floor and walls of a room (see figure 6.3).

FIGURE 6.1   Notice the straight and curved lines in the dancers' arms and legs.

FIGURE 6.2   Arabesque position.

Another way to think about line in dance is to visually trace a line or lines from one point on a dancer's body to another point. Look again at the dancer in figure 6.2. Move your eyes along this dancer's body so that you trace a curved line from the fingertips of the lifted arm to the toes of the leg in back. It is usually this long and more continuous line that attracts the most attention from observers when a dancer is in arabesque. Another type of arabesque position can be seen in figure 6.4. This form of the arabesque is called allongée. It is an elongated version of the basic arabesque shown in figure 6.2. In arabesque allongée, the back

FIGURE 6.3   Oblique body lines.

is less curved, so you can trace a straight line from the dancer's forward arms to the toes of the lifted leg in back.

Look once more at figure 6.4. You should find that first your eyes travel along the line that extends between the dancer's forward arms to her toes in the back. Next, you probably take in her support leg by letting your eyes go from her center down to her foot on the floor. Finally, you let your eyes travel upward, tracing the line from the support foot, through the dancer's center, and then to her head. Choreographers frequently use such visual lines to guide your eyes and help you see the whole picture created by a dancer's body. As you might suspect, viewing dancers in this way becomes more complicated in a group dance. The choreographer must combine dancers of different sizes and body shapes to create a picture that fits together. The lines you trace on the bodies of the dancers must, of course, complement each other as well. As a rule, straight lines go with straight body lines, and curved lines go with curved body lines.

Look at the dancers in figure 6.5. As you do this, you should find that your eyes travel from one dancer to another along the lines created by the dancers' bodies. When I look at the dancers in this photo, I find that my eyes are immediately drawn to a point on the female dancer's hip. From this point, my eyes are pulled up to the male dancer's head, down along the line of the female dancer's upper body, to her dropped arm, back to the center of this grouping, and finally down to the floor along the female dancer's support leg. Although you can allow your eyes to move around this photo in a different route, I think you can see how the placement of dancers' bodies causes you to trace visual lines in space. Dance is motion, however. Although you occasionally have a chance to view static dance poses like those in figure 6.5, you usually see a constantly changing arrangement of lines in a performance.

FIGURE 6.4   Arabesque allongée.

Your eyes are attracted to the lines created by dancers' bodies because the lines represent actual physical forces in the dancers' bodies. Return to figure 6.5, and study the two dancers again. Notice how the lines created by the bodies of the two dancers can be described with movement words. For example, the line from the point on the female dancer's hip to her dropped arm goes up and over to the side, and the line from her center down to her support foot shoots into the floor. When you describe each line using movement-oriented words, the photo appears dynamic rather than static. The sense of movement you see in the body lines copies actual physical forces in the dancers' bodies.

Before I became a dance major in college, I was an art major, and so I have been interested in the relationship between these two fields for many years. One of the similarities I discovered between visual art and dance is that each

FIGURE 6.5   Tracing lines visually on the body.

uses *visual tensions,* which are like the lines that copy the physical forces found in the bodies of the dancers in figure 6.5. Without visual tensions, a work of art looks flat and dead; visual tensions create the appearance of movement in a work of art (Arnheim 1974). Illustrations of people in action poses may capture your attention because they look real. The degree of realism in such a drawing depends on how skillfully the artist uses visual tensions. In other words, the work that looks wooden lacks the visual lines of tension that mimic the actual physical forces existing in the live human body.

An excellent example of visual tensions can be found in drawings of dancers in action. In the early part of the 20th century, many artists enjoyed drawing Isadora Duncan while she performed. These drawings tell us a lot about how Duncan danced because the artists used lines in a way that copy the actual physical forces in Duncan's body (see figure 6.6). Painter Wassily Kandinsky also produced some drawings based on the physical lines of force in dancer Gret Palucca's body. Kandinsky's drawings are more like diagrams, however, because he shows us the visual tensions without even including an outline of the dancer's body in the drawing (see figure 6.7). The point here is that the choreographer must emphasize visual tensions while making a dance. Otherwise, the dance will look static and less exciting for the audience to watch.

Another use of line in dance extends the visual lines of force out into space beyond the dancer's body. By doing so, the choreographer makes empty space

FIGURE 6.6   Drawing of dancer in a Duncan-like movement.

that surrounds the performers become part of the dance because it is energized. Empty space onstage is energized through the performer's ability to throw energy outward. Philosopher Suzanne Langer called this illusion *virtual entity* because it is created in the space around a single dancer's body and between two or more moving dancers. As a result, the choreographer creates an illusion that looks real because it is made up of the visual tensions that are an extension of the dancer's movements. In a successful dance, the physical components merge with this virtual entity so that the audience sees the dancers and the surrounding space as one.

Rudolf Laban was a 20th-century dancer, choreographer, movement theorist, and visionary who invented a notation system for dance. Laban was also interested in the reach space immediately around a dancer's body, which he called the *kinesphere.* Dancers can reach into this space with their arms and legs. This space

FIGURE 6.7   Drawing of dancer Gret Palucca by Kandinsky.

can also grow and shrink as a dancer stretches and bends the joints. The energy in a kinesphere is similar to a virtual entity, but it is created by dancers' movements as they reach into the space surrounding their bodies (Maletic 1987).

Creating Body Lines in Personal and General Space

Choose one part of your body to work with in this exploration. This body part can be your arm or leg or even your torso. Once you have selected the body part you want to work with, make three lines in space using the selected part of your body. Make sure, however, that these lines are located at different levels in your personal space. If possible, curve one of the body lines. Then, move from one body line to the next without stopping. Next, repeat each of the three body lines, but this time create the lines as you move through general space so that each one is performed in three locations. Again, move from one body line to the next one without stopping. Finally, make a drawing or diagram of each body line that you created.

Tracing Lines Visually

You can also create body lines by using your eyes to trace from one point on your body to another point. Begin by standing in front of a mirror. Next, place your body in a shape that is balanced, or symmetrical. Study this body shape in the mirror. Then, use your eyes and trace a line between two different points on your body. Repeat the process of tracing a line between two points until you have created three different lines that you can follow visually. Finally, decide whether the lines you traced with your eyes were straight, curved, or a combination of these two. Do this exploration again, but this time visually trace lines on an unbalanced (asymmetrical) body shape. Compare the lines you traced on the balanced body shape to those you created using the unbalanced shape. Were the lines you traced straight, curved, or a combination of the two?

Body Lines and Physical Forces

You will create three different shapes with your body. The first one will be at high level and contains straight body lines. The second one is at middle level and contains curved body lines. The third body shape is twisted and is at low level. Practice each body shape in front of a mirror. Then, repeat all three shapes, focusing on the body feelings you experience in each. Remember that the lines and shapes you create with your body represent physical tensions within your body.

Planes

In chapter 1 you explored the directions in which you can move your whole body or in which you can move a part of your body. Now, if you keep your body aligned so that it forms a straight line and then move this line in a direction, you are moving in a plane. Your forearm forms a straight line from the wrist to elbow, but if you move this line, it also creates a plane. The plane is parallel to the floor if you move your forearm back and forth horizontally. If you move your forearm up and down while it is still in a horizontal position, you create a vertical plane (see figure 6.8).

A *plane* is flat and two-dimensional because it has no depth. A flat piece of paper is an example of a plane, and it can be positioned so that it represents a number of planes. Thus, when the paper is held vertically and perpendicular to the floor, it is a vertical plane. When the paper is held horizontally and parallel to the floor, it represents a horizontal plane. You could even hold the paper at an oblique angle to indicate a slanted, or oblique, plane.

In chapter 2, you explored the moveable parts of your body—your joints. You also discovered that some of your joints, such as your elbow, have a limited movement potential, whereas other joints, such as your shoulder, offer more movement possibilities. The point here is that it is possible to describe the movement potential of different joints by talking about planes of movement. In fact, *kinesiologists*, people who study human movement, describe three primary, or

FIGURE 6.8   Creating a plane by moving the body line formed by the top dancer's forearm.

cardinal, planes that intersect at the center of the body. The *frontal plane*, which is perpendicular to the floor, divides the front half of the body from the back half of the body. The other perpendicular plane, or *sagittal plane*, divides the body into right and left halves. The third plane, or *horizontal plane*, divides the top half of the body from the bottom half. If you move your whole body forward, your body moves in space in the sagittal plane. Moving your whole body directly to the side describes the frontal plane. If you twist at your waist, you are twisting the upper part of your body in the horizontal plane. Movements of the arms and legs also occur in the three planes described. The planes of movement for the arms and legs do not cut through the center of the body but are parallel to the cardinal planes (see figure 6.9).

Some joints permit movement of body segments in more than one plane, and some do not. You can move your forearm at the elbow in only one plane as you bend and straighten your arm. You can move your upper arm at the shoulder, however, in all three planes: Your upper arm can move to the front and back in the sagittal plane and from side to side in the frontal plane. You can also twist your arm at the shoulder in the horizontal plane.

FIGURE 6.9   Moving arms parallel to one of the cardinal planes.

Creating Planes in Personal Space

Stand in front of a mirror, and hold your forearm up so that it creates a vertical line in space that is at a right angle to the floor. Keep your forearm in this vertical position, and move it so that your forearm describes as many planes as possible. Then, change the position of your forearm so that it forms a horizontal line in relation to the floor. Keep your forearm in this horizontal position, and again move it in space to create multiple planes. Make an oblique line with your forearm as well, and move this oblique line to describe other planes.

Creating Planes in General Space

Stand in front of the mirror again, but this time move your whole body so that the line created by your body describes a plane. You should find that moving your body straight forward describes the sagittal plane, whereas moving your body to the side creates the frontal plane. Then, if you move your body line on diagonals, you create diagonal planes. See how many different planes you can create by moving the line of your body in various directions.

Create five different planes, but use one body part to create three of these planes and your whole body to create the others. Practice moving in each of the five planes. Then, move continuously, going from one plane to the next without stopping. Change the order of the five planes, and move from one to the other again without stopping.

Group Shapes

The use of shape in dance also applies to arrangements, or groupings, of dancers. In chapter 2 the shape of a single dancer's body was described as symmetrical or asymmetrical. Groups shapes can be symmetrical or asymmetrical as well. When you consider group shapes, however, you must view the group of dancers as one unit. Thus, a symmetrical grouping is one in which the body shapes of the dancers on one side of the group match the body shapes of the dancers on the other side. In an asymmetrical grouping, the body shapes of the dancers on one side of the arrangement do not mirror the body shapes of the dancers on the other side. Of course, when you arrange dancers in groups, it is necessary to focus on movement rather than on static positions. In addition, if the dancers do pose in a group, they must retain a feeling of energy so that the grouping does not look static (see figure 6.10).

Look again at the dancers in figure 6.5. As discussed earlier, your eyes are drawn to a particular point in the grouping. For me this point is at the center of the female dancer's hip. The point to which your eyes are drawn is called the *focal point*. The focal point is also the point from which you will begin to visually explore the group shape created by the dancers' bodies. You may also notice that as you explore the grouping of dancers, your eyes are drawn back to the focal point from time to time. When you arrange dancers in groupings, you must establish a focal point for each group shape. It is also important to understand that

FIGURE 6.10   Group in back is symmetrical; group in front is asymmetrical.

straight body shapes generally go with straight body shapes, and curved body shapes go with curved body shapes. When you arrange dancers in groups it can be distracting to include both straight and curved body shapes in the same grouping.

Betty Edwards (1999) wrote about techniques she developed for teaching drawing. Her techniques are included here because they can be helpful for dancers. Edwards encouraged her students to observe more carefully whatever they were drawing by seeing shapes and relationships between these shapes. She found that once students are taught to observe in this way, they can translate what they see more easily into a drawing. Edwards' method of seeing and drawing is based on the *right brain mode* of thinking. This mode responds to wholes such as shapes, images, and pictures, whereas your *left brain mode* digests information one piece at a time. Typical left brain types of information include input arranged in a series, such as numbers, letters, and words.

You can also use right brain techniques to observe group shapes in a dance by looking at the outlines of groups of dancers, not all the details of the dancers that make up each grouping. Thus, you see groups of dancers as a whole, not as separate dancers. To help you do this, focus on the outline or outside edge of group shapes as they form and reform. This technique enables you to focus on how groups of dancers change and develop throughout a work.

Another aspect of the right brain mode of seeing involves becoming aware of relationships between shapes. The spaces between objects are *negative spaces*, whereas the objects themselves are *positive forms*. By focusing on the negative spaces, students can see whether the relationship between objects is near or far, above or below, in front or behind, and so on. If you are arranging groups of dancers onstage, you need to be aware of the relationships between the dancers. If your intent is to have the audience see a grouping of dancers as an ensemble, you should tighten the negative spaces between the dancers. Wide negative spaces cause the audience to see the dancers as individuals, not as part of one group. Large negative spaces onstage can also appear as dead space. Always be aware of the negative spaces between your dancers or between parts of a single dancer's body, and make the negative spaces part of the visual designs in your choreography. Remember that dancers can energize the space around them, so use this energy to make negative spaces come alive and be a part of your dance (see figure 6.11).

Another way to view relationships between dancers and groupings of dancers is to consider the concept known in psychology as *figure-ground*. When you view the world, some objects immediately pop out from the background. Visual separation of objects from the background is based initially on their physical differences. Visual separation is also due to the human ability to see in terms of figure and ground. The part of visual field that appears sharply defined is the figure, and the rest of the field is the background, or ground (Schiffman 1996). Other factors that determine what is a figure and what is ground are the texture of an object, its distance from the viewer, its color, and how imposing the object appears. Thus, objects that are recognized as a figure have the quality of being a thing. They are not formless. The figure also appears closer to the viewer than the ground and may be dressed in a lighter color. The figure usually looks more impressive or dominant than the ground as well.

The concept of figure-ground will help you arrange single dancers and groupings of dancers onstage. When you arrange the dancers you need to decide which dancers or groups of dancers are supposed to be the figure and which ones are the ground. Usually, a soloist or group of dancers becomes the figure if they are closer to audience or look more distinctive or dominant. Placing dancers in the center of the stage makes them the figure as well. Costuming a featured dancer or dancers in light colors or having them dance in a spotlight will also distinguish them from the ground. In any case, your challenge will be to arrange your dancers so that you get the results you want (6.12).

FIGURE 6.11   Negative spaces and positive forms.

FIGURE 6.12   The dancer in front is the figure and other dancers are the ground.

Balanced and Unbalanced Group Shapes

You need to do the following exploration with at least one other person. Begin by making three group shapes with the other dancer. These shapes should include one that is symmetrical and two that are asymmetrical. Next, look at the three group shapes in the mirror, and find the focal point in each one. The focal point is the place where your eyes are drawn when you first look at the group shape. Then, let your eyes wander from the focal point to other points in the group shape. Can you describe the pathways that your eyes follow as they move around the group shape? Were these pathways straight or curved?

Group Shape and Contour

Create three new group shapes with your partner, but this time position the shapes so that they are at different levels. Then, study each group shape by using your eyes to trace its outside edge, or contour. Finally, describe each shape in terms of its contour. Were the shapes wide, narrow, large, small, and so on? Did you find a relationship between the level of a group shape and the way you described its contour?

Negative Spaces and Positive Forms

Make three more group shapes with your partner, but this time create group shapes in which you and your partner have a different relationship in each shape. Remember that you can position your body so that you are beside, over, under, around, or reaching through parts of your partner's body. Next, look at the positive forms (that is, where your bodies are located in space) created by your bodies in each group shape. Then, find the negative spaces (that is, between body parts and between whole bodies) in each group shape. How do the positive forms change as your relationship with your partner changes? What about the changing relationship between you and your partner and the changes in the negative shapes?

Advanced Pathways

Pathway is the path traced by movements of one body part in space or by the whole body as it moves across space. In general, the pathway created by a moving body part is traced in the air, although it is possible to use your hand or foot to trace a pathway on the floor. Traveling (locomotor) movements create a pathway on the floor called a *floor pattern*. Pathways and floor patterns can be straight, curved, or a combination of these two extremes.

The idea of spatial pathway is easier to understand if you can visualize the pathways traced by the moving body or by moving body parts. In fact, dancing in a light-colored costume in front of a dark background emphasizes movement pathways, as does moving while holding a streamer or scarf. In each of these examples, the viewer will see a *tracer effect*, or afterimage, that makes the spatial pathways more visible. Holding a flashlight or having glow-in-the-dark patches on your costume can also exaggerate the tracer effect. Some contemporary choreographers have taken the tracer effect a step further by using a computer technology called *motion capture* to map dancers' movements. The result is a video recording that looks like the tracer effect (see figure 6.13).

The idea of spatial pathway was also a part of Rudolf Laban's movement theories. Laban created several large three-dimensional models to help describe the pathways through which the body can move in space (see figure 6.14). Each of these models was large enough to allow at least one dancer to stand inside of it so that the model surrounded the dancers' bodies. After designing his models, Laban created movement sequences that followed specific spatial pathways, linking one point on the model to another. Some of the movement pathways were performed at outer reaches of the model, whereas others cut through its inner space to end on the other side of the model (Maletic 1987).

FIGURE 6.13   Motion capture effect.

Reprinted, by permission, from Johannes Birringer, CORD News, 2001. "New environments: Interactive dance." CORD News 21(1): 9.

FIGURE 6.14   Three students demonstrating a three-ring form within an icosahedron.

Courtesy of Laban Centre London, New Cross London.

The floor pattern that a dancer traces on the ground is more concrete than the concept of spatial pathways. In fact, many choreographers have used floor patterns to keep a record of their dances. I can remember taking a social dance class in college in which the text contained a series of floor patterns found in the different dances taught in class. An 18th-century system of dance notation called Feuillet also used this same idea. The patterns these early dancers traced along the floor are balanced along a center line that runs from upstage to downstage. This center line divided the stage in half so that if a dancer followed a circle on one side of the stage, he moved in a circular floor pattern on the other side of the stage as well. The geometric floor patterns matched the phrases in the music (Turocy 2001).

Advanced Pathways in Personal Space

Begin by drawing three simple shapes on a sheet of paper. These shapes can be a letter of the alphabet like U or a geometric shape like a circle. Then, trace each shape in space using one body part that is on the outside of your body, such as the tip of your finger or the top of your head. You can also use each body part to trace the path formed by a selected geometric shape. Remember, however, that you are tracing in personal space only. Next, trace the same three paths in your personal space, but use a point that is located at the center of your body, such as your navel, a rib, or any other central point on your body. To end this exploration, trace the same three paths, first with the outer, and then with the central parts of your body, but do this without stopping. Was it easier to trace shapes using a point on the outside or center of your body? Why do you think this is?

Advanced Pathways in General Space

Take a look at the room in which you are moving. Next, position four large objects such as chairs or stools in this space, but scatter the objects throughout the room. Then, design a floor pattern that takes you around the room from one object to another. As you go from one object to another, lead with different parts of your body. When you get to an object, stay in one spot for a while and move by relating to the object in as many ways as possible. Then, continue to the next object by again leading with one body part. Draw a diagram of your floor pattern after you complete this exploration.

Advanced Pathways in Personal and General Space

Draw a diagram of a floor pattern that carries you around the room. Use only straight lines to create this floor pattern, however. Next, move through the floor pattern you created using two different locomotor movements. Then, perform the floor pattern again, using the same locomotor movements, but this time move both arms so that you are tracing straight paths in space at the same time. Do the same exploration using a floor pattern made of curved lines, and accompany this curved floor pattern with arm movements that trace curved paths in space.

Movement Transitions

A transition is a movement connection that functions as a link between actions. Usually you do not notice transitions between movements, but they are there just the same. For example, you worked with group shapes in the preceding section of this chapter. Now, if one group shape is high and the next one is low, a movement transition must link the shapes. The shapes are noticeable to observers, but the group of dancers must move their bodies through a pathway in space to make a transition from the first shape to the second one.

Movement sequences also make use of transitions between separate movements. Transitions act as bridges to bind movements together and give a dance continuity. Each transition grows from a movement and leads into the next movement. Transitions can be abrupt or smooth depending on the style of a dance.

A good example of a skillful use of transition can be found in some dances created by a company named Pilobolus. In one of their dances, described by dance critic Deborah Jowitt, the company members created constantly changing group shapes that looked like *M*s, a pair of eyeglasses, and double arches. The viewer's focus could shift back and forth between the designs, the dancers' moving bodies, and back to the designs again. Pilobolus members skillfully used transitions that allowed the audience to see a series of constantly changing shapes without being distracted by the movements between the shapes (see figure 6.15).

When I was teaching beginning choreography, I often noticed that some students created dances that combined their original movements with set steps (such as those found in ballet or jazz dance) in a way that caused the set steps to stand out or look disconnected from the rest of the choreography. Later, I realized that the set steps stood out not only because they were so different from the original movements but also because the dancers included the set steps without giving any thought to the transitions. Perhaps if the students had created better transitions, the set steps would not have looked so out of place in the dances.

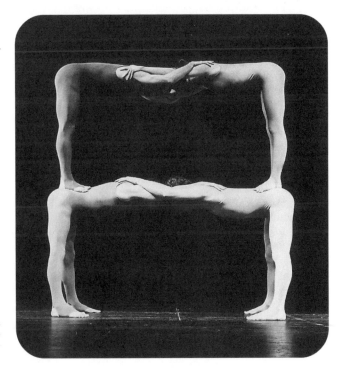

FIGURE 6.15   Pilobolus dancers.

Reprinted, by permission, from Jerome Robbins Dance Division, The New York Public Library for the Performing Arts: Ascot, Lenor, and Tilden Foundations.

Transitions Between Group Shapes

Work with another dancer and create four group shapes. Position these shapes in one spot but at different levels. Next, decide whether you are going to use straight or curved pathways to make a transition from one group shape to the next one. For

example, if the first group shape is high and the next one is low, you can transition by moving straight down to the low shape. Another choice is to go to the floor by following a curved pathway that goes out and then down to the lower shape. Then, perform the whole sequence of group shapes plus the transitions between them without stopping. Which type of transitional pathway—straight or curved—was easier to do? Why do you think this is? Draw a diagram that represents the transitions you have used to change level (see figure 6.16).

FIGURE 6.16   The drawing on the left represents movements that go from high to low to middle levels. The figure on the right represents movement change from middle to low to high levels.

Transitions Between Movement Sequences

Begin by selecting three nonlocomotor movements that you can put together to form a short movement sequence. For example, you can perform the movements reach, twist, and bend one after the other to create a sequence. Then, practice the sequence you created by repeating it at three different levels. Finally, do each version of the same sequence without stopping as you go from one level to the other. You should be able to change level easily and begin moving again by inserting movement transitions between each version of the sequence.

Transitions Between Floor Patterns

Draw a diagram of three simple floor patterns that are not connected. These floor patterns can be geometric shapes such as a circle or triangle, or they can be simple, irregular shapes. Next, move through each of the floor patterns, but use a different locomotor movement in each one. Finally, move from one floor pattern to the next without stopping. Use the same locomotor movements you used in each floor pattern, but find ways to make the transition from floor pattern to floor pattern.

Ordering Movements

Order is the placement of separate items in a sequence. Thus, finding an order for the items depends on the choices about which items come first, second, and third in the sequence. Order, however, can be based on many concepts. For instance, a list of names could be arranged in alphabetical order or according to a person's importance in an organization. Sometimes it is even possible to use a numerical order to arrange separate items in a sequence. In the case of ideas, it is usually best to choose an order that begins with simple ideas and builds to more complex concepts.

The concept of order is also important in Gestalt psychology, which defines perception in terms of units of information that a person receives. Gestalt psychologists have said that we make sense of our world by grouping input in a way that gives it order. For example, it is possible to recognize a melody as the same one whether it is played on a piano or violin because the separate notes in the melody have a particular order that we can identify. A different order of the same notes would, in turn, produce a different melody, or no melody at all.

Order is also important when you arrange individual movements or movement sequences in a dance because you must decide which movement comes first, second, third, and so on. Usually you will develop movement sequences or even sections of a dance fairly easily. You may find, however, that it is difficult to decide whether these sequences fit at the beginning, middle, or end of a dance. One way to find an order for your movements is to return to the reason that you are creating your dance. You may find that your motivation suggests a slow beginning with a low energy level and a feeling of building to greater speed and power by the end of the dance. Conversely, a different motivation might mean that you can put the most powerful movements of your dance at the beginning. The order you select for the movements in your dance depends on how you want the dance to grow and develop. A skillful use of movement order can also help the audience enjoy and connect with your dance.

Alwin Nikolais was an innovative 20th-century American choreographer. One of the many dances he created called *Tower* illustrates the importance of movement order in a dance. Throughout this piece, the performers constructed various structures with pieces of aluminum fencing. The structures the dancers built were always too small to enclose all of the dancers, however. As a result, one or more of the dancers were popped out of each structure. Finally, the dancers built a tower after they had danced with the pieces of aluminum and constructed the smaller structures. In the end, this tower was sent tottering with a flash and an explosion. The importance of the tower at the end of this dance grew from seeing the dancers move with and manipulate the individual pieces of aluminum throughout the piece. Nikolais established a specific movement order to build the expectations of the audience and connect the separate parts of the dance together.

Ordering Single Movements

Choose two locomotor movements and two nonlocomotor movements. Give each of these movements a number, then perform the four movements in numerical order. Next, give each of the four movements a new number, and perform the movements in the new order. Describe the transitions you used between each movement in both sequences. Which movement order was easy for you, and which one seemed more difficult? Why do you think one movement order was easy and the other one was more difficult?

Alwin Nikolais

Alwin Nikolais (figure 6.17) began to develop his style of dance theater after World War II. His works are experimental but easily identified through the unique blend of movement, sound, and light. Often, Nikolais extended dancers' movements through the use of costumes or props to create works filled with surprises, floating images, and optical illusions.

FIGURE 6.17   Alwin Nikolais with Hanya Holm.

Photo courtesy of Colorado College photo file, Special Collection, Tutt Library.

Ordering Movements by Concept

Choose three other movements for use in this exploration. These movements can be nonlocomotor movements or locomotor movements, but make sure that you can do one of the movements slowly, a second one at a medium tempo, and the third one very fast. Next, decide on a speed for each movement and on how many times you will perform each movement. Then, arrange the three movements in an order based on their speed, beginning with the repetitions of the slow movements and advancing to the repetitions of the fast movements. Finally, reverse the order of the same three movements by beginning with the fast actions and ending with the slow actions. This exploration is an example of ordering movement based on the concept of speed. Which movement order was easiest for you to perform?

Ordering Movements by Motivation

You will write a short story that includes a simple series of events. Next, create a sequence of movements that you can use to tell your story. Then, decide how many times you will do each movement, and arrange the movements in an order that is based on the order of events in the story. Conclude this exploration by having someone watch you perform your movement story so that you can tell whether the order of your movements matches the sequence of events in your story.

Patterns and Relationships

Many kinds of patterns exist; some are natural and others are made by humans. The clouds in the sky form natural patterns, whereas the brickwork on a building is a manmade pattern. Some patterns such as those made by the bricks are more concrete, whereas other patterns such as those found in a piece of music are not concrete objects at all. A map is a simple example of a pattern because it shows how different places are related geographically. You can describe such relationships by saying that two points on a map are close or far apart or that one is farther north than the other one. You can also look at a map and see how points on it are linked by roads.

The concept of *pattern* is about creating relationships between bits of information that form a whole (Caine & Caine 1997). These relationships can be between objects, ideas, or, in the case of dance, between movements. The point is that when you find a pattern or patterns in information, the bits of information are no longer seen as isolated. Thus, identifying patterns is a way to make sense out of nonsense and give meaning to input. Our brains resist unorganized bits of information because these bits have no meaning, and the best way to find meaning is to organize separate items so that you can see the pattern of relationships between them.

Finding patterns in information is based on research in many fields. Technology has allowed us to see the interconnected nature of our world. For example, we know that our universe is much more fluid and changeable than was previously thought. This discovery means that it is now more appropriate to discuss patterns and relationships between bodies in the universe than it was to discuss isolated bodies in space. The ability to see relationships between parts of the subject is called *sighting* (Edwards 1999). You can sight by seeing angles between objects and a horizontal or vertical plane or by comparing the size of one object to another.

Dance has many types of patterns. The floor pattern followed by a dancer is one type of pattern; it is a map that shows the relationship between the stage space and where the dancer is in the space. A pattern could also describe the use of energy throughout a dance; you can also diagram these changes in energy. You might use an upward arrow to represent light energy, a downward arrow to show a heavy use of energy, a smooth line to show sustained energy, and a wiggly line to indicate a use of vibratory energy (figure 6.18). In addition, longer lines would indicate that a specific use of energy had continued over a longer period. When viewing the whole diagram, you can see the basic changes in energy use throughout the dance and how use of energy at one point relates to or contrasts with energy use at another point in the piece.

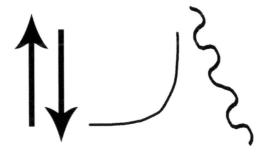

FIGURE 6.18   Diagrams can be used to describe the changes in energy that occur in dance.

When we think and learn, we actually use patterning in two very different ways. As explained earlier, first we must be able to discover patterns in bits of information that come to us. This is what we do when we see patterns in clouds or in the bricks on buildings. The second way we use patterning, however, is to reorganize information that comes to us to make new patterns. For example, to learn information for a test, a student reads the assigned chapter in the textbook. Then she can draw a diagram to show how this new information relates to the information in earlier chapters. So the student is creating a pattern of the relationships between different pieces of information.

In dance, you can use both types of patterning. When you watch a dance in performance, you see patterns and relationships between individual movements and between different parts of the dance. These patterns represent relationships the choreographer wants you to see. You make sense out of the dance by understanding its structure and by seeing how separate movements change or develop from the beginning to the end of the piece. When you create a dance, however, you create new movement patterns based on how you want the dance to look or what you want the dance to say to the audience. Consequently, the job of giving structure or meaning to the dance is now your responsibility. You must take individual movements and movement sequences and arrange them in patterns that represent relationships that highlight the intent of your dance.

Creating Spatial Patterns With Body Shapes

Make seven different shapes with your body. One shape can be narrow, another wide, a third irregular, and so on. Perform each of the shapes you created in front of a mirror. Then, using paper, cut out a shape that resembles each of the body shapes you just practiced. Now, arrange the seven paper shapes in a pattern so that they fit together. The pattern should have a focal point and a sense of unity. Create at least two other patterns with the seven paper shapes.

Identifying Movement Patterns

View a videotape of a solo dancer performing to music that has a steady underlying beat. In this performance, find a short sequence of movements you want to analyze in terms of its pattern. Look carefully at this movement sequence and draw a diagram of the pattern created by the timing of the dancer's movements. You can easily draw this diagram by relating the dancer's movements to the underlying beat of the accompaniment. For example, movements that take more time are represented by a longer dash, and movements that take less time are shown with a shorter dash or dashes (see page 35). Next, draw a diagram of the same movement sequence, but this time the pattern you draw will represent the dancer's use of energy. If the dancer's energy is sustained, you can draw a smooth line; if the dancer's energy is percussive, your line is jagged. How does the dancer's pattern in time relate to the energy pattern of the same dancer? For example, sustained movements usually take more time than percussive movements, and vibratory actions are even faster than percussive actions. Finally, draw a diagram of this dancer's use of space. The spatial diagram could be based on movement direction, level, or use of floor patterns.

Creating Your Own Movement Patterns

Begin by making a simple diagram that represents a movement pattern in terms of its energy, timing, and use of space. Then, focus on your use of energy, and duplicate this pattern with your movements. Next, focus on the timing of your actions, and again reproduce the pattern represented in the diagram. Of course, longer lines in the diagram result in longer movements, and shorter lines produce shorter movements. Finally, focus on your use of space by creating movements that follow the direction, level, or floor patterns in the diagram. Review each of the movement sequences you created, and compare them. You should be able to describe the relationships that were produced each time you reproduced the pattern in the drawing. In other words, what happened to the way you used space or energy when the timing of your movements changed? How did your timing change when the direction, level, or size of your movements changed?

Summary

Dance movement requires special attention to perception—how do the lines and group shapes you create actually *look* to someone watching the dance? Are you conveying what you mean to say? How you order movements and provide transitions between movements is also important. Movements will create patterns, and patterns can relate an idea or theme that may be difficult to express otherwise. Concentrate on these ideas and challenge yourself to move as suggested in the following improvisation exercise to convey the expression you intend.

Challenges and Reflections

Move throughout the available space using three different locomotor movements. Stop three times and make an interesting body shape each time you stop.

- Describe the outline of your three body shapes and the negative spaces you created between different parts of your body.
- Describe the order you used to perform the locomotor movements in your improvisation.
- How successful were your transitions between the locomotor movements and your body shapes?
- Select one of the movement elements—space, time, or energy—and draw a diagram that represents how you used this element throughout your improvisation. This drawing is the pattern of your use of space, time, or energy.

chapter

7

Using Signs and Symbols

otice how people stand when they are angry or upset, or when they are elated or surprised. Whether it is intentional or not, your body communicates every time you assume different body shapes and use various movements. One way to observe human movement is to look at the postures people use when they talk to one another. For example, some people lean forward when they are talking, and others pull away from the person they are speaking with. In either case, however, the posture of the person speaking says something to an observer. In the first case, the speaker appears intent and even aggressive about getting her message across, whereas in the second case the person talking looks more relaxed and removed from the person she is speaking to.

You will have a chance to look at how your movement can send a message to others. Communicating through movement is a form of nonverbal communication, which begins in infancy, but that remains a part of our lives on a daily basis. Nonverbal communication in the form of gestures helps a mother and child communicate, and it can add meaning to a politician's speech. In this chapter you will explore how movement can be used to communicate in a dance and how using movement as nonverbal communication affects your use of body shape and of the elements space, time, and energy. Creating movement sequences that communicate can be thought of as forming movements into symbols that represent your feelings or ideas. Some of these symbols are similar to gestures you use every day, and others are much more abstract. You will have the opportunity to explore both types of movement symbols in this chapter. This chapter ends by connecting the pictures you have in your mind to the movements you create. Such mental pictures are sometimes known as visual imagery.

Say It With Movement

If you say it with movement, you are using your body to send a message to others. Hand gestures are often used to get the message of our words across to a listener. For example, when you are excited, you probably speak and gesture wildly, whereas you use much smaller gestures to accompany your speech when you are calm. Gestures are not the only body language that we use, however. The whole body shapes our message in the same way our vocal cords shape our words. For example, an elderly woman can appear much younger than her years if she has the posture of someone half her age. This woman may use little effort to stand and sit, and she may have a regal posture rather than a stooped posture (see figure 7.1).

When a group of people have a common point of view, they often share the same or a similar posture. When one person in the group shifts his stance, the others in the group also change their posture. On the other hand, people who disagree tend to have different postures. The way you place your weight on your feet sends a message as well. For example, someone who is more involved in a group discussion usually stands with her weight on both feet. However, standing with the weight on one foot while leaning away from the group shows that the person is not interested in what the group is talking about. Finally, spatial place-

FIGURE 7.1   Dancer on right side has regal posture.

ment in relation to the group is also important because it can suggest how much power a person has in a group. The person with the highest rank or most power usually sits at the head of the table in the meeting room, or he stands at the front of the group.

Movements in the form of gestures can also be connected to the locale or region in which the gestures are used. Some gestures are more universal because their meaning is understood by many groups of people. For example, the raised arm indicates a request for attention. Children learn this gesture in school, but it extends to adult life and has widespread use today. A gesture that is common in southern Italy but not throughout the rest of the world is for a man to shake his tie to show that he is not fooled by the actions of another person (Morris 1994).

Five types of human movements that can communicate are emblems, illustrators, regulators, affect displays, and adaptors. Movement *emblems* are not dependent on what a person is saying because they have a direct verbal translation and are familiar to most people in a cultural group. An example of a movement emblem is the gesture of bringing the forefinger and thumb together to form a circle to show that everything is OK. *Illustrators* are used along with speech to create emphasis, but they have little meaning when seen alone. Thus, moving your hand slowly and in a horizontal direction can describe a flat piece of land. However, if you do this same gesture without speaking, it could have several meanings or no meaning at all. *Regulators* maintain and guide your interaction when you are speaking to another person or when you want to begin speaking to another person. You use a regulator when you beckon with your arm or nod your head to show that you are interested in beginning a conversation with someone. *Affect displays* such as a smile or hug are a form of emotional communication. *Adaptors* are unintentional. Usually adapters are a response to boredom or stress. To turn away from a group or to move your head and look at the ceiling can indicate that you are not interested in a conversation or are trying to relieve your own feelings of stress (Richmond & McCroskey 2000).

The idea that movement communicates is not new. Babies, in fact, use their own forms of nonverbal communication. A hungry or tired baby cries, makes fists with her hands, and moves her arms and legs about in an agitated way. Babies do not talk, but they do get their meaning across with sounds and movements. Nonverbal communication also develops when babies respond to the facial expressions or movements of an adult. Educators and psychologists are now building on a baby's natural tendency to communicate through movement. Sign language is used to help children as young as eight months express what they cannot say with words. Thus, parents and others are able to understand a baby's needs. The babies, in turn, are less frustrated because they are able to express themselves. Using sign language also seems to speed up verbal development by encouraging children to use words at an earlier age (Simons 2000).

Francois Delsarte was a French music teacher and one of the first people to analyze the many ways in which the body communicates—something we now call *nonverbal communication*. Delsarte devised a set system of gestures and body postures that communicated specific feelings. For example, a hand held with the fingers apart meant exaltation and praise, whereas the hand held with the fingers dropped down communicated abandon and giving up. Delsarte also used other parts of the body to communicate. Thus, standing with the heel of the front foot next to the arch of the back foot shows strength and independence. Delsarte's system of gestures and postures seem rigid today, but his work was an early attempt to show how the body can communicate meaning. Today, many of Delsarte's ideas are part of studies in pantomime, stage movement, and dance.

Delsarte believed that there was nothing worse than a gesture that had no meaning, and a hundred pages of text could not say what a simple gesture can say. When gestures accompany speech, the gestures add meaning to the spoken word. Delsarte also believed that no two artists use the same movements to express a similar idea, because each has a different temperament. In this sense, we can compare the performances of two ballerinas who dance the same role, and we notice subtle differences in how each performs the same movements.

Today, we are beginning to realize that the body is involved on a deep, unconscious level when we think and create. The struggle to express thoughts and ideas is accompanied, and maybe even preceded by, a body feeling. Such body feelings occur before anything is created in its outward form, so the body acts as a sounding board for persons who do creative work. It is the tensing of the body, known as *felt-thought,* that precedes the creative act. The whole person thinks and the whole person creates because there is no mind except from reactions that come from the body. In other words, the first flicker of meaning begins where mind begins—in the body (Rugg 1963).

The concept of felt-thought is commonly known today as the *mind-body connection.* To understand how we think, we must understand that the brain and body interact. And although mind is more than either the brain or the body, it is also connected to them. Research has shown that the mind is found throughout the brain and body, and the physical composition of the brain changes when we make behavior choices. Making choices, of course, is based on the meaning you see in events. Different types of experiences shape the brain in different ways because the brain is plastic, or changeable. Recent research in the neurosciences has shown that thinking and learning do produce physical changes in the brain. In fact, when you learn, the nerve cells, or neurons, in your brain grow branches that reach out and connect with other neurons. In an enriched environment with more stimulation, the brain forms more connections between neurons (Caine & Caine 1997).

One of the easiest ways to understand how the body communicates meaning is to look at how space, time, energy, and shape are used in a movement. Remember that the spatial aspects of movement are direction, level, and pathway. Thus, a dancer who is moving toward you looks more powerful than one who is moving away from you. Dancers who perform at a high level also appear more powerful than those who dance at a low level. A feeling of power is also associated with moving on a straight path in comparison to traveling in curved pathways. Fast actions are exciting, and slow movements have a more calming effect on the observer. Sustained use of energy, which is slow and continuous, is more calming as well. Sustained movements can even have a hypnotic effect on the audience, although some people find such movements boring to watch. Swinging movements are playful, and percussive actions look strong or aggressive. Wide shapes have more volume and project a feeling of power, and narrow shapes seem weak. Dancers use many variations of the movement elements all the time.

Skill in working with movement and meaning comes from a greater awareness of normal body language. Making dances also involves manipulating the movement elements so that a dance fits together, and the elements are used in a way that communicates the desired message.

Hawkins (1991) indicated that dance movement communicates meaning because it grows from an *inner sensing,* or awareness of body feelings. Making dances based on feelings requires a level of involvement that takes time to develop. You must pay attention to the body sense without being distracted by other thoughts. When you are involved in how your movements feel, you will be able to create authentic dances, or dances based on your inner impulses. There is a harmony between what you feel inside and the quality of movements you create. I believe that the audience can also connect on a deeper level when a dance is created in the more feeling-oriented way. Sometimes as I was creating a dance, the movements flowed easily, and I immediately knew the movements were right bcause they followed the intent of the dance. At other times, however, I struggled while creating, and felt as though I was simply piecing movements together. I remember that the audience sensed there was something special about the dances I created using the authentic movements; they identified with these dances on a deeper level as well.

Authentic movement can be found in many well-known dances. Such a level of feeling and meaning was what José Limón described when he discussed his creation of *Missa Brevis.* Before he created this dance, Limón had been touring Europe, and in doing so experienced the effects of World War II firsthand. The devastation he discovered in Poland made an especially deep impression on him. Limón found that amidst the ruins, the Polish people were carrying on with courage and serenity. The determination of the Polish people to rebuild and maintain their traditions touched Limón deeply, and he poured these feelings into *Missa Brevis* (see figure 7.2).

FIGURE 7.2   Limón company in *Missa Brevis*.

Reprinted, by permission, from Jerome Robbins Dance Division, The New York Public Library for the Performing Arts: Ascot, Lenox, and Tilden Foundations.

What Does Posture Mean?

Sit in a place where you can observe a variety of people as they walk by. Student unions, airports, and parks are ideal locations. As you observe, notice how people carry themselves. Do they walk with an upright posture, or do they appear to drop their weight and slouch? Notice whether the people you watch move their bodies as a whole, whether they lead with one part of the body, or whether they leave another part of the body behind. See if you can attach meanings to the body postures you observe. Does the person you have been watching look bold, timid, shy, confident, or depressed? Be as precise as possible when you find a meaning for various movements; by being precise you become aware of the more subtle aspects of nonverbal communication.

What Do Gestures Mean?

This time you will look at the gestures that people around you use. Usually, people make various gestures when they are talking, so try to focus on someone who is having a conversation. Decide whether the person's gestures look excited, bold, subdued, restrained, and so on. Then, attach a meaning to these gestures. Another way to do this exploration is to watch someone who is giving a speech on television or on videotape. Before you begin your analysis, mute the sound, and see whether you can interpret the meaning of the person's gestures without hearing the words. If you are watching a video, rewind it and play it again to see whether the meaning or meanings you got from the gestures match the verbal message.

Relating Movement Elements and Meaning

Select two feelings that are opposite in tone (for example, happy and sad, or angry and calm). Next, choose one nonlocomotor movement and one locomotor movement. Do both the nonlocomotor movement and the locomotor movement in a way that expresses the first feeling, and again in a way that expresses the second feeling. You can reach and walk as if you are happy, and you can reach and walk as if you are sad. After you do each movement in the two different ways, describe how you used space, time, energy, and body shape to express each feeling. Finally, compare your use of the elements when you expressed the first feeling to how you used the elements when you expressed the second feeling.

Symbols to Representational Movements

Symbols have meaning because they represent the objects, feelings, and ideas of life. Symbols communicate by capturing something from the real world through the use of forces and tensions that make up a work of art—in this case, a dance. Thus, understanding different types of symbols is a big part of being a dance student. First, you need to learn how to interpret the movement symbols in the dances of others. Such understanding helps you appreciate the dances of other artists and perform them with a greater sense of feeling. Second, a knowledge of symbols is important to your own creative process in dance because it helps you be more precise about creating your own movement symbols that, in turn, help the audience grasp the meaning of your choreography.

The act of using movement as a form of communication in a dance involves forming movements into symbols. For many people the heart is a symbol that stands for sincerity and love. A gesture such as placing the hand over the heart is a symbol for love as well. The tree is one of humanity's most important symbols because in many cultures it represents life or even a union between heaven and earth. Likewise, the Maypole dance is a springtime symbol of renewed life and fertility. Visual symbols can be found in most cultures from early historical times when humans lived in caves to the present day. We know, however, that dance has also served as a symbol throughout history in the form of movement rituals that are an important part of ceremonies in a culture.

Everyday movements or movement sequences can be symbols as well. Previously in this chapter you read about gestures that communicate meaning to others. The raised hand is a gesture you use to show you have a question or would like to speak. Thus, the hand raise is a simple movement symbol because it has a meaning that is recognized by others. Shaking the tie is a symbol as well, but it is not a universal symbol because it's only used in southern Italy. All symbols are more than a decoration because they communicate meaning nonverbally and can be very powerful. Consider the power represented by a nation's flag and by various forms of the cross.

Nonverbal communication between humans in the form of symbols occurs on many different levels. In other words, some symbols function more as *signs* in the form of words, images, and gestures and can be found throughout our world (Fontana 1993). Signs are a simple representation of reality. They echo the real world and give us information in a clear and precise way. Signs such as those on our highways or on a map are easy to recognize and tell us what to do at a place or point in time. On a daily basis you observe stop and yield signs and communicate with hand gestures in your attempts to understand directions or send signals. Symbols, on the other hand, communicate with more depth and intensity. Symbols are less precise and direct than signs because they represent psychological and spiritual forces. Symbols can also send a message of wisdom or tell a story that is important to a cultural group. The tree represents life or the life force, and as such it is an example of a symbol. Throughout history other important symbols such as the rainbow, moon, and sun have existed in literature, mythology, and folklore. Symbols represent how we see and interpret our reality. Ancient civilizations recognized the power of symbols and frequently used them in their religious rites. In Western civilizations, however, symbols are often dismissed, although they continue to appear with a frequency that goes against the rational world in which we think we live. The popularity of the *ankh* (an ancient Egyptian symbol), the unicorn from medieval times, and dragons from ancient legends show that we have an ongoing fascination with symbols (see figure 7.3).

Several years ago, I did research for a dance based on legends of the earth goddess. In the process of doing the research for this dance, I discovered that the same or similar characters appear as symbols in different legends. In fact, one of these characters was the hero. I also discovered other recurring, symbolic characters in my research, such as the trickster and the twins. According to psychotherapist Carl Jung, the trickster is actually an earlier version of the hero who is driven by physical needs in the same way that an infant satisfies its physical needs. The twins, on the other hand, symbolize the two sides of human nature: the introvert and the extrovert.

Many choreographers have created dances that use symbols to convey meaning. Modern dance pioneer Martha Graham used the character Thantos to represent death in the ballet *Alcestis*. In this dance, a battle for possession of Alcestis' soul develops between Thantos and Hercules, the hero figure. At the end of this dance, Hercules, who symbolizes life, wins, and Alcestis is resurrected. *Acrobats of God*, another Graham creation, symbolizes the need for perfection—a need that is common among dancers. Graham performed the title role of a

FIGURE 7.3   Ankh symbol.

choreographer who struggles to find enough inspiration to finish her dance. Many of Graham's movements symbolized her frustration and indecision. At one point in the dance, Graham even gives up her efforts and sits behind a screen. The screen is a symbol representing her desire to hide and have some peace from the demands of doing creative work (see figure 7.4).

Photo courtesy of the Estate of Arnold Eagle.

FIGURE 7.4   Martha Graham and David Wood in *Acrobats of God.*

Visual Symbols

Begin by selecting three common symbols such as a star or flag. Decide what each symbol means to you or what it says to you. It may help to think about your past experiences with each symbol so that you can focus on what the symbols mean to you. Then, choose one nonlocomotor movement and one locomotor movement. You will perform each of these movements three times. Each time you perform one of the movements, however, perform it in a way that communicates the meaning you attach to one of the three symbols. For example, if a symbol frightens you, then do the movement in a way that communicates fright. Finally, compare your three performances of each movement. How would you describe your use of space, time, energy, and body shape in each performance of a movement?

Gestures

Choose three common gestures such as waving, saluting, and shaking hands. Create a short movement sequence using the three gestures. Do this by deciding how many times you want to perform each gesture and the order in which you want to perform them. Practice your movement sequence, and then do it again, but this time change your use of one of the movement elements. If you did a normal wave first, try doing the wave high, low, to the front or back, and so on. Did the second performance of the movement sequence feel different in your body? Do you think that the second way of performing the movement sequence gave it different meanings? If so, why do you think this is so? You may want to change another movement element in the same movement sequence to see how this change affects the meaning communicated.

Think of several characters in a story or play you have read, and write a short description of each of the characters. Include descriptions of their personalities, their physical appearances, and how you think they would move. Now, create several movements that show how each character would move. The movements you create should be realistic and a pantomime of the typical actions of each character. Finally, compare your use of space, time, energy, and body shape in the movements you selected to depict each character.

Representations to Abstract Movements

A symbol is a kind of shorthand that can be used to transmit meaning; it takes the form of images, sounds, or movements. Symbols communicate because each connects with something deep inside a person and triggers feelings or memories of feelings that are the stuff of life. Symbols can be of two basic types: literal and abstract. Literal symbols are used in a work of art that includes people and objects as they look in life or that copies events as they exist in the real world. In the visual arts, a literal painting is realistic so that the people and objects look like a photo or close to it. In a literal dance, the performers also look like people moving in a real world. Literal dances also tell a story, which are sometimes called *narrative* dances because the dancers use their movements to progress from one event to another. *Pantomime* is another example of a literal movement art; the movements resemble those found in life (see figure 7.5).

Abstract symbols are much more general in nature than literal symbols. They do not look like real people or things, nor do they copy events from the real world. The Kandinsky drawing described in chapter 6 is an example of an abstract symbol because it shows only the lines of force in the dancer's body. Kandinsky's drawing captures the essence of the dancer's actions without showing you how the dancer really looked. The process of creating symbols that capture the essence of the real is known as *abstraction*.

The concept of abstraction can be difficult to understand, particularly in dance. Visual symbols are used here

FIGURE 7.5   Examples of gestures as realistic symbols.

to help illustrate this concept further. Visual symbols are easier to interpret than sounds and movements because they are more concrete and can be studied over time. Dance, on the other hand, is transitory. It is there, and then it is gone, making it difficult to remember what you actually saw. Let's begin the explanation of abstraction with color. Red can be connected with the feeling of anger, whereas blue brings forth feelings of calm or of being at rest. In this sense, red is an abstract symbol for anger, and blue is an abstract symbol for calm. Different types of lines can also be used as abstract symbols. Jagged lines look angry, and wavy lines look much more calm. Various shapes can be used as abstract symbols as well. For me, wide, jagged shapes look angry, and the more rounded shapes appear soft and calm (see figure 7.6).

Let's translate your experience with abstract visual symbols into abstract movement symbols. You can show anger by shaking your fist or by twisting your face into a scowl. These actions, however, are literal because they are from real life. An abstract expression of anger simply captures the essence of this feeling without using the typical associated gestures. A single percussive arm movement followed by a series of vibratory arm actions would show anger in a more abstract way. Here, you are using the tension or energy found in anger without performing the realistic gestures that are normally associated with anger. In contrast, you could demonstrate a feeling of calm by lying down on the ground in a relaxed pose. This pose would be very literal, however, because it is close to a real-life reaction

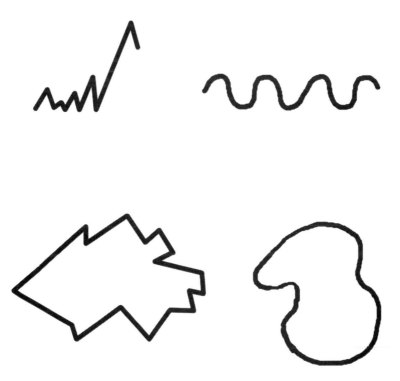

FIGURE 7.6   Lines and shapes used as abstract symbols.

to being calm. On the other hand, an abstract movement symbol that communicates the feeling of calm is to slowly and easily trace the shape of a figure eight in space with your arm.

Perhaps the key to understanding abstraction is to return to the elements of movement. In terms of space, anger is symbolized with large movements that travel in straight paths. You also use fairly rapid movements and bold strokes of energy to show anger. If you want to show that you are calm, however, you do not move in the same way. You would use smaller movements that curve and are more indirect. Your use of time is slow, and your use of energy is rather soft and gentle.

When you watch an abstract dance, you respond to both the visual forces and the actual physical tensions in the dancers' bodies. These forces and tensions form a web—a skeletal network that brings the meaning of the dance to you in a general way. This changing network is a field of forces that is hidden to the naked eye, but it influences how you respond. Looking at an abstract dance in this way is similar to the discussion of movement line, shape, and pattern found in chapter 6.

Some of the notation systems used in dance are a good example of symbols that represent abstraction in movement. One of these notation systems is called *Motif Notation,* which was created by Ann Hutchinson Guest and is made up of symbols that can be used to record many types of movements. Motif Notation captures the basic sense of a movement; it is not a record of the exact movements found in a dance. The person reading Motif Notation can create her own dance based on the basic themes or essences represented in the symbols. The exact movements on which the symbols are based cannot be re-created, however. An example of two Motif symbols appears in figure 7.7. The symbol on the left represents any movement that lengthens, reaches out, enlarges, or opens out. The

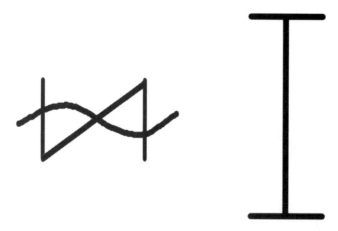

FIGURE 7.7   Motif symbols. Lengthening and reaching out (left) and straight path (right).

Courtesy of Ann Hutchinson Guest.

symbol on the right stands for actions that travel in a straight path. As you can see, these are two very general concepts that can be interpreted through several different movements. You can reach your arm out to the side; extend your leg to the back; or reach both arms to high, side diagonals to perform actions that lengthen or enlarge. You can also perform many different movements based on the idea of a straight path. You can walk or run straight forward or slide straight to the side. As I began to use Motif Notation in my own workshops, I started to see the connection between this symbol system and abstraction. The Motif symbols represent the essence of movements as they exist in the real world.

The connection between making visual symbols that represent movement is similar to a concept of *synesthesia*, which is a sensory experience that crosses over from one type of sense organ to another. If you have the ability of synesthesia you may hear music and see colors at the same time. Many children who say they feel colors, see tones, or hear visual patterns have the ability of synesthesia. Many young children view yellow as happy and brown as sad. Unfortunately, synesthesia seems to disappear with age, although many artists do retain this ability. Synesthesia is related to the human ability to use symbols: To understand a symbol you must relate the symbol to information you get from all your senses (Gardner 1994).

Literal to Abstract Movements

Write a short story that contains only one or two characters. Make sure you describe each character clearly so that your words create a visual picture of the characters. Be clear about what each of the characters is doing throughout the story. Next, create a sequence of movements that one of the characters would do in the story. The movements you select should be fairly literal or similar to those found in real life; they should also follow the story line. If you have a second character in your story, create movements that describe this character, and tell what he or she is doing as well. After you create your movements, have someone watch you to make sure he can get a sense of the characters and understand what each is doing. The movements you create are literal symbols that follow the story line and describe the character or characters. Now, focus on the characters in your story, but this time create movement sequences that represent your basic feelings about each character. In other words, you will create an abstraction of each character in movement. Do you see any similarities between your literal movement sequences and the ones that are abstract? Are the two sets of sequences similar in the way you have used space, time, and energy, and body shape?

Movement Abstraction

This exploration is designed to give you another experience with creating movement symbols through the process of abstraction. Select three pieces of music, but make sure that each piece is different in tone and quality. For example, a piece of classical music played on guitar is very different from the rhythms of jazz music and from the percussive beat of drum accompaniment. Listen carefully to each piece of music. Next, play each piece of music again, but this time scribble or draw as you listen to the different pieces of music. Do not make realistic pictures, however. Instead, make simple drawings that you think interpret the tone and quality of each piece of music in terms of the lines and shapes you use. It also helps to draw on a big sheet of paper so that you can do fairly large drawings. Draw with bold strokes, and move your whole arm from the shoulder. Drawing with a felt-tip pen helps as well. Once you have completed your drawings, set them side by side so that you can compare the type of lines and shapes you used in each drawing. Perhaps you used mostly curved lines in one drawing and jagged lines in another. Or maybe one drawing contains many angular shapes and another does not. Try to describe the type of lines and shapes you used in each drawing. Finally, play each piece of music again while you look at one of your drawings. Now begin to move by responding to the basic qualities you discovered in the music and that you reproduced in your drawing. Repeat the process of listening, looking, and moving with each of your drawings. Which drawing was easiest for you to re-create in movement? Which one was most difficult for you to re-create in movement? Why do you think it was easy for you to move in one case and more difficult in another?

Creating Abstract Symbols From Structured Movements

Select two movements—a nonlocomotor movement and a locomotor movement. Perform each of these movements in three different ways. The first time you do each movement, change your use of space; the second time change your use of time; and the third time change your use of energy. Practice each movement with the changes, and then write a short description of how each way of doing the nonlocomotor movement and each way of doing the locomotor movement looked and felt to you. In your first description of each movement, talk about your use of space; in the second description talk about your use of time; and in the third description talk about your use of energy. After you have written your movement descriptions, use a large sheet of paper to create a simple line drawing that you think is an abstract symbol for each of your movements. This means that you will have six drawings when you are finished—three abstract drawings of the nonlocomotor movement showing your changes in use of space, time, and energy and three abstract drawings of the locomotor movement showing your changes in the same movement elements. Now, compare the drawings. You should find that you created a different symbol for each way you performed the nonlocomotor movement and for each way you performed the locomotor movement.

Synesthesia

Find three pieces of paper that are three different colors. Think about how you feel about each color. For example, red may make you feel excited, and blue may be a calming color for you. Next, create three movement sequences that express your feelings about each color. Finally, think of a texture and a sound that go with each of your movement sequences. Can you find any similarities in the movements, textures, and sounds that you used to represent each of the colors?

Mental Pictures and Visual Imagery

Visual images are pictures you see in your mind. They can even be called the motion pictures of your mind. An example of a visual image in dance is to see yourself performing a leap. You can see your front leg reach forward as you push your back foot against the floor. You then see your body as you move into the air in an arc-shaped path in space. You are also able to see your front foot roll to the floor and the knee of the same leg bend to cushion your landing. This use of visualization is known as a *direct image*. You can also use visual imagery to move as an inanimate object moves, which is an *indirect image* (Overby 1990). Dancer and choreographer Eric Franklin (1996) suggests moving as though you are a cloud that changes from a flat shape to a fluffy shape. I have observed many dance teachers conduct classes, and I found that they used both direct and indirect visual images. One teacher told her students to move forward as a wave splashing onto the beach. Another teacher suggested bending the hip as if your hip were a hinge on a door. This teacher also told her students to swing their arms forward and backward like a person who was painting the inside of a large bubble that surrounds the body.

Your body image is another way to think about visual imagery. Body image refers to the picture you have of your body in your mind, which can be positive or negative. A positive body image means that you like your body or are satisfied with it. If you have a negative body image, you do not like your body or are dissatisfied with parts of your body. Your body image may also be incomplete: You may block out parts of your body, since they are not part of the mental picture you have of yourself. For example, the back of your body may not be part of your body image because you cannot see this part of your body unless you look in a mirror. Every person has many thoughts and feelings about her body that are made up of information from several sources. First, you have the visual aspects of your body image, such as its size and shape. Second, how physically aware you are of your body and its parts is important to the makeup of your body image. Thus, you may choose to pay attention to certain parts of your body, but you are less conscious of other body parts. The third component of the body image is the emotional aspect of your body image. The emotional component involves your feelings of satisfaction or dissatisfaction with your appearance or body experiences (Pruzinsky & Cash 1990). Your body image is highly personal and subjective; it can also change as your appearance changes or as you have different experiences that involve your body. Fortunately or unfortunately, your body image is intimately connected to the concept you have of yourself.

Some authorities believe that eating disorders such as anorexia nervosa can be caused in part by a distorted or negative body image. How a person perceives his weight, size, and shape is important. In other words, dancers who have eating disorders think they are fat even though they look extremely thin. Such dancers may even be obsessive about one area of the body.

The *kinesthetic body* is another way to describe body image (Houston 1997). It is a representation of your body in your brain that develops from having an awareness of different parts of your body. The size of a part of the kinesthetic body is not in proportion to the size of the same part of your real body. Instead, the importance of a part of your kinesthetic body is related to how much and in what ways you use each body part. You use your hands a lot, making them an important part of your body image. Houston believed that you can modify the kinesthetic body by increasing your body awareness. The idea of body image or kinesthetic body is not new; many cultures believe in a secondary, or less physical form, of the body. The ancient Egyptians used the term *ka*, and those who practice yoga talk about the pranic body.

Using Visual Imagery to Improve Dance Technique

You can use visual imagery in many ways to improve your dancing. An example of a simple visual image is to picture a straight line at the side of your body to help you achieve alignment. This image follows the line of gravity described in chapter 5. Anatomical images are another form of visual imagery. Use of anatomical imagery, however, requires that you know how your body is put together—the sizes and shapes of the bones, the relationship between them, and the placement of the bones in relation to muscles. The following anatomical image, developed by kinesiologist Lulu Sweigard, is intended to improve body alignment: Visualize the width of the back of the hips broadening. As the back of the hips broadens, the front of the body knits together, which makes you less likely to stand with a swayback. In this approach to imagery, however, you do no conscious movement; you simply see the back of the hips broaden in your mind's eye without moving your hips. When using visual imagery, you must also focus on a three-dimensional image, not a flat image.

You can also use picture images to correct body alignment. Some of these images may be comical, but they are based on good alignment and a sound knowledge of anatomy. Sweigard suggests imagining your pelvis is a ball of ice cream on top of a cone. Your legs, of course, are the cone. When you begin to use this image, the cone is tipped downward in front so that the ball of ice cream is almost falling forward. Next, you watch the same image as the cone moves to a level position, allowing the ball of ice cream to settle back inside the rim of the cone. This image can be used to help correct lordosis, or standing with a swayed back.

Using Direct and Indirect Images

In this exploration you will work with visual images that are both direct and indirect. We will begin with direct imagery. First, see yourself in your mind's eye while you swing your arm slowly, at a medium speed, and then as fast as possible. Then, see yourself rising from a chair and sitting down again. Finally, picture the image of your whole body as you walk across the room with a lot of energy and then with very little energy. Now, try each of these actions after you have seen yourself doing them in your mind's eye.

Now you will practice each of the following indirect visual images. Imagine the movements of a bouncing ball, a skater gliding across the ice, and the swinging pendulum of a clock. Then, move one part of your body the way the bouncing ball, the gliding ice skater, and the swinging pendulum move. Was it easier for you to move as the direct or the indirect images you just visualized? If one of the types of imagery was easier for you to use, why do you think this was so?

Working With Your Body Image and Anatomical Imagery

The following anatomical images are designed to improve your alignment and make you more aware of different parts of your body. Stand so that your feet are under your shoulders and flat on the floor with your toes pointing straight ahead. Bring your focus to your body, take several deep breaths, and concentrate on the following images. See the back of your pelvis widen. At the same time, see the front of your pelvis and the front of your rib cage narrow. Also see the distance between the bottom of your ribs and the bottom of your pelvis grow longer at the back of your body. Take time to focus on each of these body parts as a three-dimensional image. After you focus on each image, stand in place and scan your whole body. Are you more aware of any part of your body after using the images in this exploration? Next, walk slowly around the room. Does the alignment of your body feel different after you use the images?

Using Picture Images

This exploration uses picture images to help you perfect the movements that make up a sequence. Begin by practicing the following dance combination. Start on your right foot and take two steps forward. Take one more step, and then leap forward, landing on your left foot. The third step is, of course, a preparation for the push-off into the leap. Follow your leap with three skips—right foot, left, and right. End by standing on both feet as you reach up and then down to the floor. Reach up and down as quickly as you can. Practice this sequence, and then use the following picture images to refine your performance of each movement. At the beginning of the sequence, walk forward as if your body were a wedge pressing through space. As you go into the leap, imagine that your back foot (push-off foot) is a hand pressing against the floor. At the same time, reach your front leg forward as though it were a spear that pierces space. To cushion your landing from the leap, think of your front leg as a coiled spring that can give on impact. You can also improve your performance of the skip by imagining that your support leg is a spring that expands to help push you into the air. At the end of the movement sequence, move to the floor as though your body were an open fan that snaps shut. Can you think of any other picture images that you can use to improve your performance of this combination?

Observing Movement From the Inside: Selecting Movement Responses

Dancing with awareness involves more than moving in response to visual images and symbols or reproducing movements accurately in your own body by copying dance steps that others demonstrate. Dancing with awareness involves learning to feel each movement in your body as you perform it. In other words, you need to be clear about the body feeling of each movement, and dance from the inside, so to speak. The movement qualities discussed in chapter 3 describe body feelings, but in the other chapters you also translated the visual aspects of movement, such as direction and level, into body feelings. Dancing with awareness also gives your movements a vitality that aids projection during performance. It is a state that becomes automatic once you have put the building blocks in place by discovering your body on a feeling level. A more concise description of dancing with awareness is to be sensitive to the information you receive from your body. Many dancers develop a high degree of body awareness only after they have trained for many years. Dancers who have a high degree of body awareness can move easily in many directions, perform intricate floor patterns, and reproduce complicated body shapes. Body awareness is also a state in which dancers are conscious of the location of their bodies and the relationship between their bodies and the outside environment.

Dancing with awareness begins with the body, or kinesthetic, sense. Unfortunately, the kinesthetic sense is often forgotten, so we usually talk about only five senses: sight, hearing, smell, taste, and touch. Perhaps that is why many people do not connect with their bodies on the most basic level. I became fascinated with the kinesthetic sense in a kinesiology class that was part of my undergraduate dance studies. The professor of that class asked us to do the following exercise: Close your eyes and reach your arms out to each side. Bring the tips of your forefingers together without opening your eyes. This exercise is a simple kinesthetic awareness test, but when I performed it, I realized for the first time that there is a connection between moving with accuracy and the kinesthetic sense.

At the most basic level, the kinesthetic sense is a group of structures in your body known as *proprioceptors*. Proprioceptors are the minute sense organs that give you information from within your body, whereas the term *kinesthesis* refers to information that comes from your body and from your body's movements. The kinesthetic sense also includes the reflexes that help you stand in an upright position and let you know when your body is vertical, horizontal, or somewhere between these two extremes. More specifically, the proprioceptors comprise receptors near and inside joints, muscle spindles, Golgi tendon organs, skin receptors, and receptors in the inner ear. The joint receptors give you information about exact joint position, and the *muscle spindles* let you know when a muscle is active or contracting. The muscle spindles also provide information about how fast your muscles are contracting and whether your muscles are being stretched. The Golgi tendon organs send signals about the amount of force or tension in various parts of a muscle (see figure 7.8). The skin receptors are in most areas of your skin. They give you information about pressure, temperature, and touch at the surface of your body. The receptors in your inner ear detect head movements and are sensitive to the position of your head in relation to the pull of gravity, making them important for maintaining balance. Taken together, the receptors of the kinesthetic sense help you perceive the position and movements of your body, maintain your balance, and reproduce rhythmic patterns. You also use the

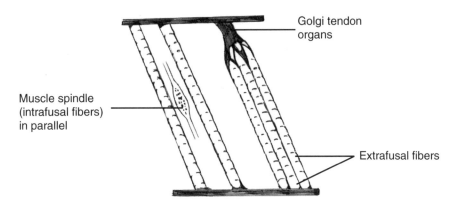

FIGURE 7.8   Proprioceptors.

kinesthetic sense to detect differences in movement effort, speed, size, and direction. Thus, movement accuracy and awareness depend on the kinesthetic sense. Above all, in order for kinesthetic sensations to be useful, they must be integrated with other forms of sensory information.

The ability to move with awareness and purpose helps you make dances because you can determine whether the body feelings generated from your movements match your inspiration. In other words, you can tell whether a movement feels right to you. To move with awareness and sensitivity, you must form a connection between your mind and body that allows you to use movement in the same way a poet uses words or a painter applies paint to a canvas.

The link between the body feeling of a movement and the inspiration for that movement can be described with the use of a *kinesthetic image*. Such an image describes the body feeling that accompanies an action (Overby 1990). You have been exploring many kinesthetic images throughout this book, such as the suspended feeling of a leap and heavy feeling of a collapse. Kinesthetic images can be both direct and indirect. Direct kinesthetic images involve actions that have a particular feeling, whereas indirect kinesthetic images suggest using actions that have the same feeling as a moving object that is outside your body. An example of a direct kinesthetic image is to move your arm with a heavy feeling. Moving your arm with the feeling of a heavy stone rolling down hill is an example of an indirect kinesthetic image. Kinesthetic images can help you refine your movement skills and choose movements appropriate for the inspiration of your dance.

It is important that you learn to focus as you practice the explorations and improvisations described in this book; it will make you aware of the kinesthetic feelings that arise from your body. One of the first steps in being able to focus, however, is learning to relax. If your body is always tense, it is impossible to be aware of the changing nature of your kinesthetic feelings. Thus, a high level of tension blocks out your awareness of more subtle body feelings. But relaxation does not mean being drowsy or falling asleep; you need to stay alert so that you can tune in to the body feelings generated by your movements. I use the words *one with* here because they describe this type of mind-body experience. When you are in a "one with" state, you can ignore the distractions around you and focus on the important aspects—the kinesthetic feelings—of your movement experience.

When you are focused, you are also in a state of *relaxed concentration* (Hawkins 1991), wherein you go beyond an ordinary, conscious state of mind because an automatic forming process takes over. Through this process you scan your movement experiences during exploration and inspiration. Movements also begin to connect so that you automatically organize and form movements into a dance. Students who achieve relaxed alertness learn best because the mind is relaxed, yet attentive. During relaxed alertness, students are challenged in a positive, non-threatening way, leading to curiosity and flexibility in solving problems (Caine & Caine 1997).

The following description is an example of learning dance movement using relaxed concentration or relaxed alertness. The dance sequence is a step to the left on the left foot, followed by a fan kick (a motion that traces a semicircular path in space with the right leg). The sequence ends when you put your weight on your right foot, placing the ball of your left foot on the floor behind your right foot and collapsing your upper body forward. You can learn this movement sequence by focusing on counts or by thinking about individual actions. You can also learn this movement sequence by using imagery and relaxed concentration or relaxed alertness. To use relaxed concentration, focus on the body feelings you experience in each part of the sequence. For example, the side step at the beginning feels narrow and two-dimensional, whereas the fan kick feels more expansive, rounded, and smooth. The collapse at the end of the sequence feels heavy as you drop your upper body toward the floor. To use relaxed concentration or relaxed alertness while you make dances, you must be constantly aware of your kinesthetic feelings throughout the exploration and improvisation. Also, you are neither too tense nor too relaxed. Such awareness helps you get involved with the essence of your inspiration and connect this essence to kinesthetic images.

Focusing on Kinesthetic Feelings

Create a short movement sequence that is made up of several nonlocomotor movements. Perform this sequence several times using the following kinesthetic feelings or images. These images include melt, dart, wiggle, bounce, and soar. Compare your use of space, time, energy, and body shape as you used the different images as your inspiration.

Transforming an Inspiration Into Kinesthetic Feelings

Select a human-made object or object from nature as your inspiration. Look carefully at the object, noting its appearance and how it feels to your touch. If you can, pick up the object to get a sense of its weight. Next, make a list of movement-oriented words that describe your inspiration. For example, *broad* and *sharp* describe objects and can be easily translated into movement. Finally, create several movement sequences based on the movement-oriented words. Which aspects of your inspiration were easy to work with, and which aspects were more difficult to capture in movement?

Connecting Kinesthetic Feelings and Inspiration

Create two movement sequences that include contrasts in direction, level, speed, energy, and body shape. For example, in the first sequence you may dance at a high level, and in the second sequence at a low level. Practice the movement sequences several times. Describe how each sequence felt in your body. In other words, write a description of the kinesthetic images. Finally, think of an internal inspiration that could cause you to move as you did in the first movement sequence and also in the second sequence.

Summary

How you move conveys how you feel. By using gestures and other visual and kinesthetic cues, you can put a particular meaning or concept into movement. The key to working with imagery, or any of the other inspirations, is to focus. Some call this level of focus relaxed concentration. During relaxed concentration you are tuned in to your kinesthetic feelings as you connect with visual images in your mind, which develops body awareness, or sensitivity to feelings that arise from your body in response to your inspiration.

Challenges and Reflections

Look in an art book and find a realistic painting that you like that conveys a story or message. You will use this painting to create images and symbols. First, find three movement gestures that tell the story found in the painting. These gestures should be literal and like the movements of pantomime. Next, create three movements with your whole body that are an abstraction of the story in the painting. To do this, focus on the basic feeling or feelings you get from the painting. After you create the gestures and body movements, weave them together to form a longer movement sequence. Think of one visual image and one kinesthetic image that describe the movements you created in this improvisation.

- Describe how you used the movement elements of space, time, energy, and body shape in your three gestures.
- Describe the changes in your posture as you performed the three abstract movements.
- Describe your use of line, shape, pathway, and pattern in the abstract movements.
- Explain why you chose the visual and kinesthetic images. What aspects of your movements caused you to think of these images?

chapter

8

Finding Sources
of Inspiration

The creative process in the arts is an amazing undertaking. When you begin, you have nothing but a vague glimmer of what you want to create. But by the end of the process you have an artistic work, or product, that can take many forms such as a painting, sculpture, dance, music, book, play, or architecture. The challenge is becoming comfortable with the creative process so that you are able to use it in a variety of situations. By learning how to convert information that is outside your body into movement, you can more easily incorporate those ideas into dance movements. For example, as I sit in front of my computer I can see pictures on the wall; hear the sound of doors slamming in the distance; and feel the smooth, concave surface of the keys on the keyboard. All of these bits of information come to me from outside my body in the form of visual, auditory, and tactile sensations. You can convert all of these sensations into movement. Thus, the shining glass covering the pictures becomes smooth, gliding movements; the slamming door becomes percussive actions; and the concave keys can be transformed into the downward curve of a swing.

In this chapter you will have a chance to look at the creative process in more detail by working with input that is outside your body. Such input is sometimes called a *motivation* or *inspiration* for movement. You will also work in greater depth with *movement exploration,* a strategy that will help you understand the creative process and do creative work in dance. You have been working with movement exploration throughout this book, but here you will read about and work with movement exploration in a more complex way. Movement exploration begins with a framework that involves an inspiration, a response to the inspiration, use of your imagination, and the result—movements—you create. Up until this point you have been using fairly simple forms of inspiration in the exploration framework. Some examples of these simple motivations include line, shape, energy, and pattern. Now you will work with more detailed sources of inspiration such as painting, sculpture, music, literature, drama, and architecture. Your response to the more complex sources of inspiration will be based on the *simple* sources of inspiration. Thus, you will begin to explore a painting or piece of music in terms of the lines, shapes, energies, and rhythms it contains; you will base your movement responses on the simpler components. As a conclusion to each section of this chapter, you will focus on the symbols you find in a work of art. In chapter 7 you read about symbols that are realistic (literal) and symbols that are nonrealistic (abstract). Now, you will use the symbols you see in a painting or hear in a piece of music as the source of inspiration for movement exploration as well.

Visual Arts

You will use the visual arts as a source of inspiration by looking at various aspects that make up a visual work of art. You are already familiar with many of these components. A painting, for example, contains many types of lines. Some of these lines are straight, some are curved, and some are a combination of the two types of lines. Some paintings include more straight lines, and some include more curved lines. It is also possible to use your eyes to trace different types of lines from one point to another in a painting. Figure 8.1 shows a pen-and-ink drawing. As you look at this drawing, you can use your eyes to trace many different lines from one point to another. The point your eyes go to first, of course, is the focal point, which is located at the approximate middle of the drawing. From the focal point, I find that my eyes curve up and diagonally to the right and back down to the center. From here, my eyes trace a line that curves diagonally down to the left, around to the right, and back up to the center of the drawing. In a sense, I have used my eyes to trace pathways in the drawing. You may be able to trace other pathways in this drawing as well.

Use of group shape is also important in the visual arts. Sculptures and paintings often include a group of objects or a group of people. Usually the people or objects that make up the grouping fit together and have a feeling of unity—they look as if they belong together. You can also look at the outside edge of a grouping (its contour) and follow this outline with your eyes. The people or objects in the grouping make up positive shapes, and the openings between them are negative

FIGURE 8.1   Pen-and-ink drawing.
Courtesy of Sandra Cerny Minton.

spaces (see figure 8.2). Some of the figures or shapes may be more prominent than others. The girl at the foreground of the sculpture is the more prominent part of the photo in figure 8.2. She is the figure, and the group of children are the less important part that make up the background, or ground.

FIGURE 8.2   Sculpture with positive forms and negative spaces.
"Like Petals Unfolding," © Dennis Smith, Clay Hill Corp.

It is also possible to find different textures and rhythms in a painting or piece of sculpture. When you use texture as the inspiration for your movement, you need to imagine how the painting or sculpture might feel to your touch. Look again at figures 8.1 and 8.2. The drawing in figure 8.1 seems to have a smooth texture to it, whereas the surface of the sculpture in figure 8.2 looks rough. A visual rhythm is also created when you look at a painting or sculpture. Remember that in dance, rhythms are created when you move faster or slower than the underlying beat of the accompaniment. You also create a rhythm when you are silent or still for a number of beats and then begin to move again. When I use my eyes to trace various lines on the drawing in figure 8.1, I find that some of the lines are long, and some are short. For instance, the first line that curves diagonally upward stops in the upper-right portion of the drawing. This line stops again as I trace back down to the center of the work. These two shorter curved lines are followed by a longer curved line that goes down to the left, around, and back to the center. The rhythmic pattern I have traced becomes short, pause, short, pause, long, pause. You may find that you can use your eyes to trace other rhythmic patterns in this drawing.

What about the symbols in figures 8.1 and 8.2? The many shapes in figure 8.1 are an abstraction of human faces and forms of many types. In fact, some of these faces and forms appear to be male, and some appear to be female. Some look quite young, and others appear to be much older. Nevertheless, these forms are symbols for human beings who have various roles in life. The symbols in figure 8.2 are more literal. For me, these symbols represent children at play. This sculpture by Dennis Smith is titled *Like Petals Unfolding*. This title could suggest that the sculptor had a deeper and more abstract meaning in mind when he created this work, however. Navajo sandpaintings also include many symbols that contribute to their meaning. The Navajo depict aspects of nature (such as thunder, clouds, hail, and wind) as people in their sandpaintings to symbolize the close connection between humans and nature (Griffin-Pierce 1992).

You can use the drawing in figure 8.1 and the sculpture in figure 8.2 as an inspiration for movement by focusing on the components of line, pathway, shape, texture, and rhythm. When you trace a straight line with your eyes, you can make straight lines with one body part or with your whole body. To translate curved lines in a work of art into movement, you can make curved lines with one part of your body or with your whole body. Likewise, you can use your eyes to trace straight or curved pathways in an artwork. These pathways can inspire movements that follow a straight or curved pathway in space or on the floor. Group shapes can also inspire movements. If the shapes in the work of art are wide, you can move by using a wide body shape; if the shapes in the artwork are narrow, you can use narrow body shapes. You can also use balanced body shapes when the shapes in the work of art are balanced and unbalanced shapes when the shapes in the artwork are unbalanced. In addition, you can translate negative spaces and positive forms into movement by showing similar relationships among parts of your body and between your body and the body of another dancer. You can even work with the concept of figure and ground if you are creating a dance with a partner or with a group.

Now let's consider texture and rhythm. For me, the smooth texture in the drawing in figure 8.1 inspires sustained movement, whereas the rough texture of the sculpture in figure 8.2 motivates bumpy, or vibratory, actions. Finally, the rhythmic pattern you trace with your eyes can motivate you to perform the same rhythmic pattern in movement. Remember, the rhythmic pattern I saw in the drawing in figure 8.1 was short, pause, short, pause, long, pause. You can easily reproduce this or any other rhythmic pattern by stepping in place, moving one part of your body in personal space, or using steps that travel across the floor in general space.

Finally, let's look at how you can translate the symbols you find in a work of art into movement. To do this, you need to decide on the meaning or meanings you find in each symbol. In figure 8.1 some of the forms look more powerful than others. In particular, the faces near the center of the drawing look forceful and seem to dominate the whole drawing. But the form at the lower left looks young and rather gentle, whereas the form at the top left appears to hover over the group or even embrace them in a protective way. When you interpret the symbols in a work of art, you also need to focus on the visual images that come to mind. Then you can translate these images into kinesthetic feelings. Remember that different images cause you to move in different ways. Of course, if you are creating a dance that uses a work of art as the inspiration, you need to weave all of the components into a unified whole. The whole dance also needs a beginning, middle, and end; good transitions; and a skillful arrangement of dancers and movement sequences.

Line and Pathway in the Visual Arts

Find a book that contains reproductions of several paintings. Oversized art history books are useful in this exploration because the reproductions are large enough so that you can see them from across the room. Select a painting that you want to work with in this exploration, and make sure this painting has a variety of colors, shapes, and details. Now, look at the types of lines you see in the artwork you selected. Are these lines straight or curved? What about the pathways you trace with your eyes as you look at the painting? In other words, when you start at the focal point of the painting, where do your eyes travel throughout the painting? Create a short movement sequence using one pathway and at least three lines you found in the painting. Was your body straight or curved in this exploration? How did the pathway you found cause you to move in space?

Shape in the Visual Arts

Look again at the painting you used in the previous exploration. This time, however, find at least four shapes in the painting that you can use as an inspiration for your own movements. Study the shapes carefully, and describe each one as best as you can. For example, are the shapes large, small, wide, narrow, geometric, or irregular? Begin moving by making the four shapes with your body. Next, place the four body shapes at three different levels and in four different places in the room. Finally, go to the location of one of the shapes and make this shape with your body. Keep this body shape as you move to the location of the second shape. When you get to the second shape, move into it, and again maintain this shape as you move over to the location of the third shape. Repeat this process until you have reproduced all four shapes and provided the transitional movements between them. Also vary the pathway between each shape, and move without stopping throughout this exploration. Was it easy or difficult for you to find movement transitions between the body shapes? Were you able to move continuously throughout this exploration? If you were not able to move continuously, why do you think this was so?

Pattern in the Visual Arts

Return once more to the painting you used as your inspiration in the two preceding explorations. This time, however, let your eyes explore the painting by tracing a pathway that extends throughout the entire work. Decide where you traced long lines, where you traced short lines, and whether your eyes stopped at any points as you traced the pathway through the painting. Remember that the way you use your eyes to trace a pathway around a painting creates a rhythmic pattern that can be translated into movement. Now, draw a simple diagram of the pathway you found in the painting by using broken lines that go in different directions or that are different lengths. Finally, translate the diagram you have drawn into as many nonlocomotor and locomotor movements as possible. You should end up with a rhythmic pattern that you can perform several times with one part of your body or your whole body or while traveling across space. Was it easier to use nonlocomotor movements or locomotor movements to create your rhythmic pattern?

Symbols and Images in the Visual Arts

You can use the same painting you used in the preceding three explorations, or you can find another painting to work with in this exploration. In either case, study the painting you selected, and pick out two figures or shapes that capture your attention. If you are working with a realistic painting, you will recognize these shapes as humans, animals, or plants. If you use an abstract painting, the shapes you select will be geometric shapes, swirls of color, or irregular forms. Carefully study the two shapes you selected. Then, decide on the meaning depicted in each of the shapes. You may even find that one or both of the shapes are a symbol for a story or series of events. Next, focus on each shape one at a time to see if it brings any visual images to mind. Finally, concentrate on the meaning of the shapes and images you discovered, translating these meanings and images into several movement sequences. You should be able to perform these movement sequences without stopping. Did the movements you created feel right to you? In other words, did the kinesthetic feelings you experienced match the meaning or meanings you found in the painting?

Rhythms and Music

Many components in music can be used as a source of inspiration. First, most pieces of music are based on a series of rhythmic patterns. You can easily describe these patterns by finding the basic underlying beat, or pulse. Some of the sounds you hear last the same length of time as the beat, and some are longer or shorter than the pulse. A piece of music may also have silences, but these silences help create rhythmic patterns too.

Melody, another important component of music, is a series of tones in a piece of music. Sometimes the tones in a melody have a high pitch, and sometimes they are low. At other times the tones of a melody fall between these two extremes. In either case, the tones in a piece of music are organized to create a forward progression. In a piece of music the tones are played in a specific order to create a particular melody. The melody is a prominent feature in a piece of music—the part most people hum, whistle, or think of when they identify a song. *Harmony*, on the other hand, is produced with more than one tone simultaneously. *Dynamics* is another common musical term to describe energy—loud versus soft, many instruments versus just one, and slow versus fast (remember from chapter 3 that dance also uses this term to describe energy). Dynamics in music also refers to how much energy musicians use to perform a musical selection. For example, music performed in a *staccato* manner means that the musicians use a fast and somewhat percussive energy quality, whereas a *legato* composition requires musicians to use smooth connected notes to sustain energy. Of course, tempo (time) is an important component in music. Tempo simply refers to the speed at which a composition is performed. Musicians also talk about *timbre*, or *tone color*, which refers to the different types of sounds that musicians have at their disposal. A painter can choose among different colors to create a painting. In the same sense, a composer can use the sounds of a violin, flute, trombone, piano, and drum to create a piece of music. Each of these instruments has a different quality, or color, that can be identified. The sound of a flute is delicate compared to the sound of a drum, and you can make a fuller sound on a piano than you can with a violin.

As in dance, a piece of music also has a form that unfolds from beginning to end. The *form* in a piece of the music is its development and organization through time. Form is the framework for the music; and as in dance, musical form is determined by the motivation for the piece. Other similarities exist between dance form and musical form, as well. For example, a piece of music may have more than one part with transitions between the parts. A piece of music is also made up of short sequences of notes that are like the short sequences of movement in a dance.

It is possible to discuss music as a symbol or as a series of symbols. Musical symbols are usually abstract, however. The only music that is truly literal has words that tell a story. So the sounds you hear in a piece of music capture the essence of a story or feeling rather than function as a literal representation of it. A polka feels jolly, blues are mournful, rap is jarring or harsh, and a lullaby is soft and soothing. A *tone poem*, in fact, is a piece of music in which the tones reflect visual images, describe characters, or tell a story. *The Planets*, composed by Gustav Holst, uses specific tone colors to suggest places in the real world, whereas *Pictures at an Exhibition* by Modest Mussorgsky is based on a set of paintings (Teck 1994). In both of these pieces of music, the sounds are abstract symbols for specific places or things. Of course, some musical selections are created with the purpose of being part of a story, or a narrative. The music composed for a classical ballet is an example of music created to support a story. Classical ballet music by itself is abstract, but it does change in tone and quality as the story of the ballet progresses.

The ballet *The Nutcracker* is a good example of how dance and music can work together to tell a story. This ballet opens on a Christmas scene with a beautiful tree and many guests at a party. Then, a mysterious, old man named Herr Drosselmeyer arrives and gives the children gifts, including the most important gift, a wooden nutcracker. At the end of this scene, the party winds down and the guests leave. In scene 2, it is late at night, but Clara, one of the children, steals back into the room, where she is treated to a parade of dancers who represent mice, snow, and sweets. The remainder of the ballet takes place in a fantasyland in which the nutcracker comes to life. As the story of *The Nutcracker* unfolds, the music changes in tone. The accompaniment during the party expresses excitement and anticipation. When Herr Drosselmeyer arrives the music turns mysterious and a little ominous. In scene 2 the music changes with the entrance of each group of fantasy characters. The mice dance to sinister music and the snowflakes to fluttering, whirling music. Scene 2 also includes Spanish dancers, who represent hot chocolate and dance to Spanish-sounding music.

It is fairly easy to translate the rhythms of music into movement. Simply listen to the music and find the steady, underlying beat, or pulse; each beat will take up equal time. The beat, in turn, is divided into groupings (called *measures)*, so that in 4/4 time there are four beats to a measure, and in 3/4 time there are three beats in each measure. You can tell how many beats are in each measure of music by looking at the top number in the time signature at the beginning of a piece of sheet music. You can also identify the measures by listening for the *accents,* or points of emphasis, at the beginning of each measure. Then, you can identify the rhythmic patterns by listening for sounds that take more or less time than the underlying beat or leave out some of beats. Accented beats also contribute to a rhythmic pattern, so be aware of the accented beats as well. Finally, translate these sounds into movements that have the same patterns and that use the same accents.

A melody is produced by sounds that vary in pitch; a specific melody must use these sounds in a particular order. So you can translate melody into movement by changing level and by using a specific order for your movements. In music, dynamics, as described earlier, is based on how energy is used. So to convert musical dynamics to movement dynamics, you need to decide on the type of energy that is appropriate for the music. For example, you can use bouncy movement to capture the feeling of a polka, and use sustained movement for a lullaby. Tempo is probably the easiest musical component to translate into movement; you simply change the speed of your movements to match the tempo of the music. Finally, you can represent tone color of music by selecting different movements to correspond to each instrument. Thus, you can use light, fluttering movements to depict a flute and percussive actions for a drum.

As indicated earlier, a piece of music has a form that includes a beginning, middle, and end; it may be made up of several parts. When you create a dance based on a piece of music, you need to understand the musical structure first.

One way to do this is to compare the rhythmic patterns, melody, dynamics, quality, and tones used in one part of the composition to those used in another part. Sometimes the same sounds and rhythms are repeated throughout a composition. At other times, sounds change or may be repeated at a particular point in a composition. A piece of music can also have transitions between parts, and the transitions may include a different use of the musical elements as well.

Although music is abstract, it does bring images to mind. Whether these images are literal or abstract, you can use such images to create movement for a dance. Translating visual images into movement means using space, time, energy, and body shape in a way that communicates the meaning connected to a particular image. A piece of music can also cause you to think of a series of images that tell a story, and you can translate these images into a movement story, or narrative, as well.

Musical Melody and Pattern

Select a piece of music that is familiar to you and that you like. This music should also have a steady underlying beat. Next, listen to the entire piece of music. Select three or four measures of the music you want to analyze in greater detail. To do this you need to decide how many pulse beats are in each measure of the music. Now, listen again to the measures you selected, and identify one or two rhythmic patterns. Describe the changes you hear in the melody. Does the melody go up, down, or stay at the same level? Is it repeated or does it change? Finally, move in both personal and general space, duplicating the rhythmic patterns you hear. At the same time, copy the changes in pitch that occur in the melody by changing the level of your movements. Repeat the same exploration with different music. Then, compare the movements you created based on the first piece of music to the movements you did with second piece of music. Which piece of music had more changes in melody and rhythm, and therefore required you to have more variety in your movements?

Dynamics and Tempo in Music

Select another piece of music for this exploration. Listen carefully to the music you selected. Next, choose a small section of the music, and listen to this section again. Describe the use of dynamics and tempo in this section of the music. Then, use two different locomotor movements and travel throughout general space. As you perform the locomotor movements, copy the use of energy and tempo you discovered in the music. Do this same exploration with another piece of music, but make sure that the second piece of music is very different in quality and tempo from the first one. Finally, compare your use of dynamics and tempo in each part of this exploration. Which piece of music was easier for you to work with? If one piece of music was easier for you to work with, why do you think that this was so?

Tone Color and Form in Music

Choose a different piece of music for this exploration. This piece of music should be short. Listen carefully to the whole musical selection. As you listen, decide how the piece develops. For example, does the selection begin fast and end slowly, and are the same melodies repeated? How do the dynamics vary throughout the piece? Listen to the tone color produced by the composer's use of specific instruments. Then, come up with a visual image or images that connect with each part of this piece of music. These images are your interpretation of this music. Write a description of the images you visualized, making sure you note the order in which each image comes to mind. Review each of the visual images, and create movements that communicate the essence, or basic feeling, of each image. Finally, perform the movements you created without stopping. To do this you may need to develop transitions between the movements. What connections can you find between a point in the music and the mental image you created to go with that point in the music? What about the connection between a point in the music and the movements you created to go with that part of the music?

Literature

Many components in literature can be used as an inspiration for movement. A book or poem is made of many words, and words can serve as a motivation for movement. When you pronounce a word aloud, the sound of that word has a specific quality similar to the tones that make up a piece of music. To my ears the word *hello* has an open quality, whereas the word *no* is more closed and abrupt. You can also change the quality of words by saying them loudly, softly, or with a particular feeling such as joy or anger.

When words are put together in sentences, they create rhythmic patterns. Read the following sentence aloud and think about the rhythmic pattern formed by the words: "If you have any questions, please call me." When I read this sentence, I find it has a definite rhythmic pattern. The words before the comma connect, or run together. Then, there is a pause at the comma, and the last three words are said with a slight hesitation after each word. I would describe the rhythmic pattern of this sentence as long, pause, short, short, short. Of course, you could say the same sentence in several ways to produce other rhythmic patterns. When you speak, you naturally stress certain words, but you do this without really thinking about it. This use of stress gives spoken language a rhythm, but it also makes it difficult for those from another culture to learn to speak a foreign language. Poets often use words in a way that creates rhythmic patterns. Thus, rhythm is a natural device for poets. Of course, one way to create rhythm in poetry is to stress certain words. Poets also create rhythm by counting the number of syllables in each line. Japanese haiku is a form of poetry that creates rhythm with a specific number of syllables in each line. When it is reproduced in English, haiku has five syllables in the first line, seven in the second line, and five in the third line.

Characters are usually found in a piece of literature as well. They come in all shapes, sizes, and physical descriptions. Most characters play a role in a story—some are good, some are bad, and others may be neutral. As the plot evolves, a relationship develops between the characters. These relationships can be between family members, friends, and associates; or they can be between characters that just happen to be in the same place at the same time. In any case, the characters can relate to each other in a variety of ways.

A piece of literature also has a form, or development through time, so that there is an order, or progression, of events. This progression of events is called the *plot*. The sense of time in literature, of course, exists in the reader's imagination, as does the sense of space and place. When you read a book or poem, you probably visualize the time and place of each scene to help you understand the development of the plot. A good writer, in turn, helps you visualize each part of a book or poem by including descriptive words in the text. Energy and timing are also part of the development of a story. Some stories begin slowly and develop to a fast pace at the end, whereas others begin with a bang and wind down until you reach the end of the story. An interesting book is also punctuated with changes in the plot, making it difficult to put down.

Literature is full of symbolism as well. One way to look at the story of Adam and Eve is to say that it symbolizes the relationship between men and women. It can also be interpreted as a symbol of how we look at sex. Another story, "Seagull's Box," is a legend of the Haida people of North America. This is the story of a gull that was the custodian of daylight. The gull took such good care of daylight that he kept it locked up tightly in a box. In the end, a raven tricked the gull into letting daylight out of the box. The raven did this by getting the gull to step on a thorn. Then, the raven needed daylight to see so that he could remove the thorn from the gull's foot. So the gull had to open the box and daylight escaped. The gull could be interpreted as a symbol of someone who is busy with his own agenda and, as a consequence, cannot see what is really going on in the outside world (McVickar Edwards 1995).

It is fairly easy to translate words and word patterns into movement. Loud words can be interpreted with large, expansive movements; soft words can be interpreted with smaller movements at a low level. Words also have feelings connected to them. You can use an open, wide movement to say "hello" and a sharp, closed movement to say "no." Even neutral words such as *table* take on an emotional tone when you say them by using a different tone of voice. For example, you can say "table" by raising your voice at the end of the word, or you can say "table" and drop your voice. In the first example, you might interpret the pronunciation of the word with a jump, and in the second example you could collapse to the floor. Finally, the rhythm of phrases or sentences can be translated directly into movement. Simply identify the rhythmic pattern of the words and reproduce it in movement.

The easiest way to use literary characters as an inspiration for movement is to write a description for each character. You can think about how the characters might look and how they move. You can also analyze each character's role. Once you have written a description of a character, you can choose gestures and postures that communicate what this character is all about. So a good character probably uses open gestures that reach out to others, whereas a bad character gestures in a much more closed way. The posture of a good character is also more upright, and the bad character probably hunches over and sneaks around. The movements used to show the relationship between characters are also important. In this sense, the more aggressive character can move toward or over the weaker character, whereas the weaker character can back away and try to hide. Remember that you can show relationships by moving over, under, beside, around, and through other dancers or objects.

Aspects of form and development in a piece of literature can be translated into movement as well. For example, as a story develops, the writer paints a picture of the place in which the story takes place. Vast, open plains can be translated into large movements that glide across space, whereas the interior of a cramped cabin requires the use of small, restrained actions. If the pace of the story is fast and energetic, you can use fast and energetic movements; and when the pace is slow, the movements can be quiet and calm. Of course, the movements you use must be presented in an order that fits the order of events in the story.

Many pieces of literature contain symbols. You read earlier about the story of Adam and Eve and also about the legend "Seagull's Box." The story of Adam and Eve can be described as a symbol of the relationship between men and women, and "Seagull's Box" can be interpreted as a symbol of someone who is so busy he does not realize what is really going on around him. Thus, to depict the characters in either of these stories, you can use movement in a literal way by using gestures and postures that are close to those used in real life. You can also create an abstract version of these stories by using movements that capture the essence of the characters or the essence of feelings expressed in the story.

Word Sounds and Patterns in Literature

Select a short poem for use in this exploration, and read it aloud. As you read, emphasize certain words, and pause between some of the words as well. Reading the poem in this way creates rhythmic patterns. Now, clap the rhythmic patterns that you created when you read the poem aloud. Do this several times, and then copy the same rhythmic patterns in movement. Remember that you can copy a rhythmic pattern by stepping in place, moving your upper body in personal space, or by traveling across the floor in general space. Next, think about the accents (emphasis) that you placed on each word as you read aloud. Add emphasis to your actions by using larger or more forceful movements at specific points in each rhythmic pattern.

Gesture, Posture, and Relationships in Literature

Choose a short story for use in this exploration. This story should have more than one character and contain descriptions of the way the characters move and interact. Read the story, and select two characters you want to use as an inspiration for your movements.

Next, create as many movements as you can think of that depict the first character. Do the same thing for the second character. When you are creating these movements, use gestures, body postures, and locomotor movements to communicate who the characters are and what the characters do in the story. Then, put the movements you have created together so that you have a movement sequence for the first character and a sequence for the second character. Perform the movement sequences for each character, and think about how you and a partner could move to demonstrate the relationship between the characters. The movement relationships should, of course, reflect the relationships of the characters in the story. In "Seagull's Box," for example, I see the raven's movements as rather cunning and stronger and larger than the seagull's. I also think the raven would move over and around the gull.

Interpreting Symbols in Literature

You can use the same short story in this exploration as you used in the preceding one, or you can choose another story to work with. But this time as you read the story, focus on the message. What symbols do you find in the story, and what do these symbols mean? Next, create movements that you think communicate the symbolic message in a literal way. These movements will be pantomimic—that is, like movements from real life. Perform the literal movements one after the other, using the order of the story to determine the order of your movements. Now, create another set of movements based on the same story, but this time focus on the overall meaning of the story. The movements you create this time will be an abstraction of the symbols you find in the story. Perform the second set of movements, but make sure the movements are arranged in an order that follows the story line. Which set of movements was easier for you to create, the literal movements or the abstract ones?

Drama

Many elements make up a play, and some of these are similar to those found in literature: character, action, ideas, language, music, and spectacle. A *character* has qualities that cause him or her to stand out. Thus, a character has needs and problems that lead to action. The character of Nora in Henrik Ibsen's *A Doll's House* is an example of a compelling character. All of Nora's actions lead to the conclusion of the play, in which she leaves her husband and cuts off all contact with him. So all of Nora's problems and involvements throughout the play lead to the action she takes at the play's end. Therefore, the ideas in a play develop from the actions. The idea of a play is sometimes referred to as its *theme*, which is a lesson learned or a helpful behavior that can be applied to real life. The theme is more abstract than characters and actions, but it is something that audience members can remember about the play (Hatcher 1996).

Language is what the characters say onstage; it depicts a play's action and meaning. Of course, some movements onstage are not accompanied by words, but even these actions are usually preceded or followed by language. Words are important, but the way a character says the words also reveals the story in a play. Actors can give meaning to words by changing the tone, volume, and rhythm of the words. In a sense, an actor's use of language creates an image or series of images for the audience.

Music and spectacle are essential to a good play. *Music* can be actual music that accompanies part of a play, or it can be sounds that are important to the action. There is no music in *A Doll's House*, but certain sounds are an important part of the action, such as the thud of the door closing and the click of the latch as Nora leaves. *Spectacle* is what is seen onstage. It can refer to actions onstage such as a swordfight or dance number, or it can be props, costumes, or movements of the technical equipment. Character, action, and idea are in literature as well as in drama. The main difference is that in live theater you can see the characters perform their actions onstage and hear the rhythm and tone of their words. When you read literature, you must imagine the actions of the characters and the rhythm and tone of their voices. You can also imagine sounds and visual elements when you read, but in live theater you actually hear the sounds and see the special effects.

Creating movements that represent a character or the actions of a character is similar to creating these movements when you read a book. Movements based on a theme are also similar to movements that are created to convey a story. You can, of course, create a literal representation of a character or theme or produce an abstraction of these two elements. To create movements based on the actor's language, you can listen to the tone, pitch, volume, and rhythmic patterns in the actor's speech. You can ask yourself whether the tone is forceful or timid and whether the pitch is high or low. The volume of an actor's words can be communicated through the use of large movements to indicate a lot of volume or small movements to indicate very little volume. Movement representing sounds that are part of a play is the same as creating movement based on the different sounds in a piece of music. Again, you can ask yourself about the tone, pitch, and rhythmic organization of the sounds to determine the movements you will create. Some sounds such as the thud of a door or the click of a latch also send a message that is connected with the play, and those messages can be helpful in creating meaningful movements as well. Spectacle is a combination of visual elements and onstage movements. Movements that represent the visual elements in theater can be based on aspects of the visual arts discussed at the beginning of this chapter. These aspects include line, shape, pathways, and visual patterns. Colors used in costumes and sets are also a part of the visual elements onstage. Movement explorations that use the actors' movements as the inspiration can focus on how the actors use the elements space, time, energy, and body shape.

Character Analysis in Drama

Get a videotape of one of your favorite musicals for use in this exploration. From this video, choose a five-minute clip that shows one of the main characters in the musical as he or she talks and moves around the stage. Watch this clip several times. The first time you watch, notice the gestures and postures of the character. The next time, listen carefully to the character's voice. And the third time you watch, look at the colors, lines, shapes, and patterns on this character's costume and on the set. Finally, write a description that includes elements of the character's movements, voice, and costume, and aspects of the set. Review your description of the character, and create a sequence of movements based on this description. What aspect of the character was easiest for you to work with? Why do you think that this was true?

Dramatic Theme

Begin by watching the entire video of the musical that you used in the preceding exploration. As you watch, keep a record of the story line. After you finish watching the musical, describe the various themes or the lessons learned from this production. Then, write down one or two words that you think communicate the essence of each theme or lesson. Finally, create a sequence of movements that is based on the words you wrote. The movements you create will be an abstraction of the themes or lessons in the musical. Perform all of the movement sequences you created without stopping between them.

Architecture

Architecture is a very rich source of movement inspiration. When you first look at a building from the outside, however, its shape probably impresses you the most. Buildings, of course, come in many shapes and sizes. Individual homes are often small and rather squat, although they can be thin as well. Skyscrapers are usually tall and thin. It is interesting to note that many modern commercial buildings have taken on more exotic shapes today. Churches of various denominations have their own unique shapes that reach toward the sky.

Remember that when you move a line in space, it moves through or forms a plane. Planes are flat and two-dimensional. So it is possible to look at the outside of a building and see many planes. For example, the outside walls of a square or rectangular building form vertical planes that are set at right angles to one another. Buildings that have flat roofs or balconies have many horizontal planes. A building with a peaked roof, on the other hand, has a roof that is made of diagonal planes. Some buildings even have walls set at diagonal angles to each other.

You can also find many lines on the facade of buildings. Again, these lines can be straight, curved, or a combination of the two. It is also possible to trace many types of lines on the facade of a building by moving your eyes from one point on its surface to another. The architect, in fact, designs a building so that your eyes will follow a particular path when you look at the building. In the case of a skyscraper, your eyes usually move up toward the sky along the vertical lines. This emphasizes the height of such buildings. Other buildings are designed to emphasize their horizontal lines so that your eyes trace a path that moves from side to side (see figures 8.3 and 8.4).

Pattern is another aspect of architecture. Patterns are created on the surface of buildings in many ways. For example, the placement of windows on a building creates a pattern that is sometimes sparse and at other times busy. Patterns can also be created through the use of brickwork and pieces of wood placed one against the other. The relationship between the bricks or between the pieces of wood creates a pattern, however. Also, various ornamental designs are put on the surface of a building to contribute to the overall pattern. An architect uses such patterns to break up the visual surface of a building and make it more interesting

to the observer. Thus, patterns on buildings create texture for the eye. You can also walk up to a building and get a sense of its texture by touching it. Bricks usually feel rough, whereas metal can feel smooth (see figure 8.3).

Lines and patterns also create a visual rhythm on a building. Look again at figure 8.3. This building has both vertical and horizontal lines that cause your eyes to go up and down, and also back and forth. The series of windows on the building in figure 8.4 creates a rhythmic pattern that combines horizontal and vertical lines. On this building, the vertical lines are longer than the horizontal lines that outline most of the windows, so the rhythm here is short, long, short, long repeated over and over. Can you find any other patterns on the building in figure 8.4?

Another way that you can use architecture to inspire movement is to think about your relationship to the architecture. For example, you can have several relationships to a building. If you are outside the building, you can be in front, at the side, or behind the building. You can even be on top of a building, although most of us do not climb on top of a building unless we go to the observation deck of a skyscraper. If a building is very large, you feel

FIGURE 8.3 Note the vertical and horizontal lines on the Cathedral of the Immaculate Conception in Denver, Colorado.

FIGURE 8.4 Note the pattern of vertical and horizontal lines on East High School in Denver, Colorado.

dwarfed unless you are far away from the building. Now, if you move inside a building, you usually feel protected and enclosed, although sometimes the inside of a building can give you claustrophobia. You can also change your relationship when you are inside a building. If you lie on the floor, you see a room from a different vantage point than when you are standing up. Standing on a chair or table gives you another perspective from which to view the inside of a building. Finally, you can look at a building as a symbol, but to do this you need to decide what a building means to you. For example, many bank buildings are constructed in a large, square shape, which gives them a sense of power and security. Private homes, on the other hand, are designed in shapes that look more comfortable and inviting.

It is possible to translate the components of a building into movement. In chapter 5 and at the beginning of this chapter, you explored movements based on lines, planes, shapes, and patterns. The challenge in this section is to observe these same components as you look at a building, and then explore them in movement. The tactile aspects of a building can also be translated into movement. People can have various relationships to a building, as described earlier. To explore such relationships in movement, think about how you feel about being at different places in a building. Then, you can show these relationships by moving with another dancer or with an object. Remember, when you move in a relationship, you can move in front of, behind, and at the side of other dancers or objects. Moving in a relationship also involves moving over, under, around, and through dancers or objects.

Lines, Planes, Shapes, Textures, and Patterns in Architecture

Find an interesting building in your city. This building should have a variety of lines, shapes, and patterns on its facade. You can also use a photograph of a building in this exploration, but it is better to work with a real building. First, describe all the lines you see on the surface of the building. Second, note the contour or outside edges of the building. What is the overall shape of this building? Can you see any other smaller shapes that form parts of this building? For example, many buildings have a small roof over the porch that creates an interesting shape. Third, how many planes make up this building, and how are these planes connected to one another? Do the planes meet at right angles, or do they form other kinds of angles? And are the planes vertical, horizontal, or slanted? Finally, touch the building, and look at the patterns on the surface of the building. How do the textures feel, and can you find any rhythmic patterns in the visual patterns? After you study the building, use the exploration framework and create several sequences of movement that represent your favorite lines, contours, shapes, planes, textures, and patterns. Try to go back and forth between the different design elements on the building so that the resulting movements are woven together in each sequence. In other words, do not simply focus on one component such as line, but go back and forth between the various components as you create your movements.

Relationships Between Buildings and People

Go back to the room in which you have been moving throughout the explorations in this book. This time, however, put yourself into different positions in the room. You can lie on the floor, stand on a chair, or sit in a chair. You can also place yourself in different parts of the room such as in the middle, near the doorway, or in one of the corners. Select four different places in the room. Then, move around the room, stopping in each place so that you can experience it fully. Next, think about how you felt when you were at the different places in the room. Using these feelings as your inspiration, begin to move and explore. For example, you can move low to show that you are on the floor or small to show that you are scrunched in a corner. You may also use movements that extend over or surround an object to show that the room surrounds your body. Again, come up with several movement sequences that express your feelings about the relationship you experienced in each place in the room.

Architecture and Abstraction

Choose three different buildings in your city, and go to each building. First, walk around the outside of the building so that you get a sense of what the building is like from this vantage point. Notice how the building looks and whether it has any distinctive features or decorations. Then, go inside the building, and walk around the interior. Again, notice colors, decor, lighting, room size, and so on. After you have inspected all three buildings, choose several words that describe how you feel about each one. Also note whether you feel differently about the inside of a building in comparison to its exterior. For example, many times I thought that a house with a rather cold exterior was surprisingly comfortable and warm inside. Finally, create three sequences of movement that represent your sense of both the outside and inside of each building. In other words, you will create an abstraction of each building.

Summary

Anything can be inspiration—visual arts, rhythm and music, literature, drama, and architecture. By exploring the components of each in a literal or abstract form, you are ready to take that knowledge and create movements based on your own senses and inspirations. The improvisation exercise that follows is only one way to practice this concept.

Challenges and Reflections

Choose a book or short story that you read recently. Review this story in your mind by thinking about the characters, the setting, and the plot. Now, select one character in this story and place this character at a specific point in the development of the story. Focus on the character and the point in time. Think about the actions of this character and imagine how he or she looks. Be as detailed as possible by painting a mental picture of the character's face, eyes, hair, and clothes. Imagine how this character moves as well. Then, imagine how this character sounds when he or she speaks. Does the character speak loudly or softly, with an accent, or in a rhythm? Next, take your mental focus to the environment that surrounds this character. For example, is the character on a beach, in a large room with a fireplace, or surrounded by trees in a forest? Try to imagine some of the textures that are in this environment. Finally, after you paint a detailed mental picture of the character and the surrounding environment, begin to move and explore different aspects of the scene you imagined. You will use your imagined visual images, sounds, words, movements, and the environment as the inspiration, or motivation, for your movements.

- Describe how you worked with the visual aspects of your mental images or pictures. Did you focus on colors, lines, shapes, or patterns when you did your movement exploration?
- How did you work with the words and sounds you imagined? What aspects of the words and sounds did you use as the motivation for your movements? Remember that different words and sounds vary in terms of dynamics, tempo, tone color, and rhythmic pattern.
- Were you able to imagine how the character in your story moved and what type of gestures he or she used? If so, what aspects of the imagined movements did you use as inspiration in your exploration?
- In what type of environment did you place your character? For example, did you focus on natural forms such as grass and trees, or did you imagine an urban environment filled with buildings? How were you able to use this environment as an inspiration for movement?
- Do you think that the movements you created are literal, abstract, or a combination of the two?

chapter

9

Creating Your Own Dances

Congratulations! You've learned the fundamentals of movement. You've been inspired to explore your environment and be creative in your expression. Now it's time to put it all together. This chapter will guide you with nine easy-to-follow steps for choreographing your own dance. By following these steps, you can create hundreds of different dances. The "Your Choice" and "Connections for Reflection" sections will help you expand previous improvisations to create whole dances that relate to your inspiration.

You should find that as you move through this chapter, your mind and body connect and reconnect in the dance-making process. For example, you use your mind to identify your source of inspiration, but you involve your body when you improvise. Table 9.1 shows the nine steps in the dance-making process and the connection that the step has with either mind or body.

TABLE 9.1 Use of Mind and Body in Dance Making		
STEP 1:	Identifying your source of inspiration	Mind
STEP 2:	Identifying movement responses	Body
STEP 3:	Creating phrases	Body
STEP 4:	Finding order	Body
STEP 5:	Varying movement sequences	Body
STEP 6:	Creating structure	Mind
STEP 7:	Designing your dance	Mind
STEP 8:	Observing your dancers and dance	Mind
STEP 9:	Preparing for performance	Mind

Step 1: Identifying Your Source of Inspiration

Your source of inspiration is where you begin to create your dance. You have already explored and improvised using many different sources of inspiration. It is possible to describe sources of inspiration as external and others as internal. An example of an external source of inspiration is a painting, piece of music, or object from nature. An internal source of inspiration is a body feeling, memory, or belief. External sources of inspiration exist outside your body, whereas internal sources of inspiration are a product of your mind and body.

To create, you need to become a keen observer and be highly involved with your inspiration. Observation is an important thinking tool that creative people use. Famous painters such as Georgia O'Keefe are an example of how artists observe their inspiration in a way that contributes to the uniqueness of their work. O'Keefe suddenly realized how to look at a flower by observing many details such as its outline, shapes, and variations in color (Root-Bernstein & Root 1999).

Several years ago, I created a dance based on Wassily Kandinsky's paintings—an external source of inspiration. To create this dance, I studied Kandinsky's paintings carefully, noting his use of color, line, shape, visual paths, and patterns. I also tried to understand the symbols he used and whether any of the paintings contained a message. The following two descriptions are examples of how the internal inspirations—memories and beliefs—were the inspiration for a dance. Graham created many of her dances with a female heroine as the central character. Many of Graham's dances are a series of solos; the action focuses on one or two people. The dignity displayed by the Graham heroines was based on Graham's belief that women can exist independently, just as men do (Siegel 2001). Alvin Ailey's work is another example of how dances can reflect the memories, experiences, and beliefs of the choreographer. Ailey grew up in southeast Texas; consequently, many of his dances reflect the repression he felt living a segregated life. But other Ailey dances project the pride he had in the African American church, or the special feelings he had for his mother.

Your Choice: Identify Your Source of Inspiration

1. Select a source of inspiration from the following list.

   External Sources of Inspiration

   Painting
   Sculpture
   Rhythms and music
   Literature
   Drama
   Architecture
   Objects from nature (flower, leaf, shell, feather)

   Internal Sources of Inspiration

   Body feelings
   Memories
   Images
   Beliefs
   Symbols

2. Once you have selected your source of inspiration, study, observe, and think about it in detail.

3. Decide which components of the inspiration you want to use as the starting point for creating movement.

4. If you selected a natural object, painting, or sculpture as your inspiration, study it carefully. Notice its color, shape, texture, planes, and whether it has any lines or patterns on its surface.

5. If you selected music, focus on the underlying beat, rhythmic patterns, melody, dynamics, tempo, and overall form of the selection.

6. If you selected a story, poem, or play, focus on the sound and rhythms of the words, the characters, use of symbols, and the overall form.

7. If you selected a memory, belief, or symbol, take time to focus on this inspiration. Form images in your mind that are related to the inspiration. Use details of the images such as colors, shapes, textures, patterns, and sounds to inspire your movements.

8. Clarify the feelings you have for the inspiration you have selected or the meaning you attach to it.

9. Which aspects of your inspiration will you use as the basis of your improvisation in the next section?

Step 2: Identifying Movement Responses

Identifying possible movement responses also requires you to be highly involved in the process of exploring and improvising. It means knowing how your movements look and how they feel in your body. Moving in this way is sometimes called dancing with awareness.

Identifying movement responses includes matching your body feelings with the components of your inspiration. Involvement also suggests a certain level of focus and concentration that some call relaxed concentration. In this state, you are able to focus on sensations as they arise from your body because your mind is alert. At the same time, your body is relaxed enough to move and respond with a variety of actions. Once you have identified possible movement responses, you can select those that are right for your dance.

Your Choice: Identify Movement Responses

1. Review the selected components of your inspiration.
2. Position yourself in a space so that you can move freely.
3. Stand quietly and focus on your inspiration.
4. Decide whether you will use your whole body or only a part of your body, and decide how your body is supported.
5. As you improvise, focus on the use of space, time, energy, and body shape that is right for your inspiration. For example, is it more appropriate to move at a high level or low level? Should your use of timing be fast or slow? Is your energy sustained or percussive? Are your body shapes wide or narrow?
6. Be aware of the floor patterns you are using.
7. As you improvise, visualize whether your dance will be a solo, a partner dance, or a group work. You can also create a dance by relating to an object.

8. Select the movement responses that have the same body (kinesthetic) feeling as the components of your inspiration.

9. Review your selected movement responses and decide whether they fit the inspiration for your dance.

Step 3: Creating Phrases

A movement phrase is the smallest unit of overall form in a dance. In dance, a phrase is similar to the phrases that make up sentences when you write a paper. It also has a sense of form because it grows (has a beginning), builds (has a middle), and comes to a conclusion (has an end). It takes many phrases, however, to make up an entire dance. All the phrases in a dance should not be the same length or be put together in the same way. For example, when all the phrases in a dance are eight counts long, the organization of the dance becomes overly predictable. The use of phrasing is also predictable if each phrase begins with an impulse and ends with a drop in energy, because the dynamics of the phrases are the same. All the phrases in a dance should relate to the inspiration for your piece as well.

The use of your breath is one of the simplest ways to help you understand movement phrasing. You can create breath phrasing by using the inhalation and exhalation of one breath as the motivation for a single phrase. Thus, as you start to inhale, you begin to move, reaching the middle of the phrase as you finish inhaling. The end of the phrase is the point at which you finish exhaling. You can perform breath phrases with one part of your body or with your whole body. You can also use energy to help you understand movement phrasing and serve as a motivation. Remember that energy propels, or causes, your body to move. Therefore, when you apply energy to your body, you begin a movement phrase. When your energy dies, the phrase ends, only to start up again to create your next movement phrase. If you use very little energy at the beginning of your movements, your phrase is rather short. If you use a lot of energy at the beginning, your phrase is longer, unless you stop abruptly.

Several other examples may help you understand movement phrasing. Remember that nonlocomotor movements occur in personal space and include actions such as swinging, reaching, and stretching. You can create another type of phrase by adding several nonlocomotor movements together. For example, if you reach high and then let your arm drop and swing from side to side until it no longer has enough energy to move, you have created a movement phrase. You can also create a movement phrase by adding several locomotor movements together. If you perform two skips followed by four running steps, you have created a longer movement phrase.

A final way to look at phrasing is to look at body shapes and the transitions between them. Imagine three body shapes that can be described in the following way. In the first shape, your body is at a high level and you are leaning to the right. In the second shape, you are bent down close to the ground. In the third shape, you are at a high level again, but you are leaning to the left. Now, if you move continuously from the first shape through the second shape and end in the third shape, you create another movement phrase.

Your Choice: Create Phrases

1. Perform the movements you discovered while you improvised.
2. As you perform the movements, decide how you can shape these movements into phrases, or small units, of movement.
3. Can you use your breath or changes in energy, or simply add several of your movements together to make a phrase?
4. Create three or four phrases.
5. Do your phrases match the body feeling you had for your inspiration?

Step 4: Finding Order

You develop longer sequences of movement or an entire dance by linking movement phrases together. The challenge, however, is deciding on an order for the phrases and providing movements that act as links, or transitions, between them. Sometimes the order of phrases comes about in a natural way when you improvise, but the creative process can also work in mysterious ways. For example, you may discover phrases that are appropriate for the end of a dance before you discover the phrases for the beginning of the same piece. At other times, you need to consciously select and arrange phrases in an order that is right for your dance.

Remember that sometimes transitions are noticeable, and at other times they blend with the phrases before and after them. The most important point is to arrange phrases and transitions in an order that suits the inspiration for your dance, communicates the right message, and matches the images you have in your mind.

Choreographer Paul Taylor created a work titled *Brandenburgs* (see figure 9.1). There is a section in this work in which the male dancer dances with the three female dancers. The male dances with each female dancer one at a time, creating distinct sections in this piece. In other words, the male dancer's movements used to change partners do not blend in because the transitions are easy to identify (Mazo 2000).

Your Choice: Find Order and Link Phrases

1. Select five or six of the movement phrases you created.
2. Decide whether you want your transitions to be noticeable or whether the transitions should blend with the phrases.
3. Experiment with the order of your phrases until you have a longer movement sequence with an order that suits the inspiration of your dance.
4. Create actions that link your movement phrases.

FIGURE 9.1   *Brandenburgs* by Paul Taylor.

© Johan Elbers 2003.

Twyla Tharp *on choreography*

Choreographer Twyla Tharp created many dances that seemed unplanned to observers. Her dancers sometimes looked as if they were about to crash into one another, but they never did. Often, Tharp's dancers moved in parallel and intersecting pathways or over and under one another in a haphazard way. At other times, Tharp's dancers performed the same movements at different places on the stage and used different movements in the same stage area. Thus, Tharp's dances were put together in a way that looked spontaneous, but they were actually very carefully choreographed. One of the reasons these dances looked so spontaneous is that transitions between phrases and between sections of the dances blended with the rest of the movements. This use of transitions suited the style and motivation for many of Tharp's dances. (See figure 9.2.)

FIGURE 9.2   Twyla Tharp Dance Company in *Eight Jelly Rolls*.

Reprinted, by permission, from Jerome Robbins Dance Division, The New York Public Library for the Performing Arts: Ascot, Lenox, and Tilden Foundation.

Step 5: Varying Movement Sequences

Movement variation is another important aspect of dance making. Through variation, movement sequences can change so that you can extend your dance and make more out of less. Varying movement sequences allows the choreographer to include them a second time or even many times in a dance without being too repetitious. You can use the elements space, time, energy, and body shape to vary movement sequences. Remember that space includes the aspects of direction, level, and size. A dancer's use of space can also refer to pathways in space and floor patterns. Time can be fast, medium, or slow; and when you move at different speeds in relation to a pulse, you create a rhythmic pattern. Energy qualities include sustained, percussive, vibratory, swinging, suspension, and collapse. You also explored light and heavy energy and free and bound flow earlier in this book. Body shapes provide many possibilities for movement variation—they can be wide, narrow, tall, short, and so on. You can also vary your movement sequences by using different parts of your body and by supporting your body in a variety of ways. Moving in a spatial relationship to an object or to another dancer or dancers can add variety to your piece as well.

Your Choice: Vary Movement Sequences

1. Can you do your movement sequences in different directions?
2. Can you perform your movement sequences at different levels?
3. Can you change the pathway of your movement sequences?
4. Can you perform the same movement sequences using different energy qualities?
5. Can you use different movement speeds to perform your sequences?
6. Can you perform your sequences using different parts of your body or using supports in different ways?
7. Can you do your movement sequences in a relationship with an object, other dancer, or dancers?
8. Make sure the variations you create fit your inspiration.

Step 6: Creating Structure

You must link many movement sequences together to create a dance, but you must use linking in a way that creates even longer sequences of movement, or parts of a dance. The parts, in turn, must add together to create a whole. The whole refers to the overall organization, or structure, of your dance. A way to understand the concept of a whole is to imagine the United States as one country, or the whole. Individual states make up parts of the whole. Many rivers in the United States extend from one state to another and act as links between the states.

The Mississippi is an example of a river that flows through or along the boundary of at least 10 states.

When you make a dance, you use your sense of time to create a whole; the dance develops through time. For example, your mind creates a whole from a series of events that have a relationship in time. The events may be grouped together because they mean something to you. Your memory of an event is usually tied to people or places and to other events that happened before, during, or after it. For example, I can clearly remember the day of my college graduation as a whole, or capsule, in time. I remember my parents arriving at the university, going to the sports pavilion for the ceremony, and returning to the dance building for a reception afterward. Thus, this series of events is tied together as a whole in my mind.

In a dance, the ongoing patterns of movement are seen as the overall form of the dance in time, or its whole. The whole dance, of course, is based on more than simply adding movement phrases and sequences together because the whole dance is greater than the sum of its parts. Experiencing the whole means looking at relationships and connections rather than seeing the parts of the whole in a fragmented way. The whole has traits that do not exist in any of the parts. Form is the organization of forces in a dance based on its structure. There is something special about a dance that has a sense of being a whole. Such a dance has a feeling of vitality, as though the dance were coming into being. The form in such dances is described as organic (Hawkins 1988).

Alma Hawkins

Alma Hawkins (figure 9.3) founded the UCLA Dance Department, the first separate dance department in the U.S. at a major university. She was a pioneering dance educator, particularly in her writings about creativity. In discussing dance in education, Hawkins, also a dance therapist, drew many connections between dance, psychology, philosophy, and the other arts.

FIGURE 9.3 Alma Hawkins.

Courtesy of California Regents: UCLA University Archives, Powell Library.

The idea of a whole is important in a dance because the choreographer's concept of the whole gives a dance its form. The dance can be organized in many ways, but it will look like a jumble of isolated movements without the unifying effect of overall form. The overall form, of course, is determined by the intent of the dance, so it is important to keep your inspiration in mind during the creative process. So the form you choose for a literal dance is not the same as the form you use for an abstract piece. The style of your dance can also affect its form. For example, the organization of movement in a lyric dance is different from the organization of movement in a jazz-style work, resulting in a different form for each piece.

When I teach beginning choreography, I begin the class by talking about the connection between dance form and meaning. I believe that the overall form of a dance is its container in much the same way a plate holds a salad or a cup holds coffee. The material in a container can have many tastes and textures, but the container needs to fit the quality or texture of the content. In essence, you do not usually eat salad from a cup or drink coffee from a plate, because each container has a different purpose. In my choreography classes, I also explain that in the beginning, dance making is easier if you use some rules to define the overall form of a dance. One of the most basic rules is that a dance has a beginning, middle, and end.

The overall form of a dance springs from many sources. Graham usually commissioned music for her dances, but it was the choreographer and not the music that determined the form used in a piece. Graham expected a composer to follow her script or outline of action when creating the accompaniment. Graham also listened to each section of the music as it was written so that she could make sure it fit her ideas for the form of the dance. Thus, in a Graham choreography, the form grew from the story or drama that she wanted to communicate to the audience (Mazo 2000).

George Balanchine was artistic director of the New York City Ballet for many years and one of the most influential choreographers in the United States. Balanchine followed a different path than Graham did when he gave form to his ballets; music was the inspiration for many of his works. Balanchine created the first part of *Concerto Barocco* by visualizing the two violin solos in J.S. Bach's *Double Violin Concerto* as two female dancers. The melody line of the two violins mingled, causing Balanchine to see the two dancers as equals (Jowitt 1988). Later, in the largo section of the same concerto, the tones are deeper, and the melody of the second violin flows under the melody of the first violin. At this point, one of the female dancers leaves the stage and is replaced with a male dancer.

Using your right and left brain is another way to create dances and form them into a whole. The right and left brain modes of thinking allow you to absorb and work with information in different ways. Remember that left brain thinking is linear, whereas right brain thinking is global. Thus, if you switch from using the right brain mode to using the left brain mode, you shift from thinking in a timeless way to thinking in a logical, step-by-step progression. In right brain thinking the emphasis is on seeing and understanding the overall form of your dance. In left brain thinking you work with ordering movements, phrases, and sequences one at a time. The ability to use both your right and left brain is important to your success in dance making. The following paragraphs contain some helpful hints about how you can shift back and forth between these two modes of thought.

You can strengthen the connection between the right and left brain modes of thinking in several other ways. You can use both visual and verbal cues to help you use both your right and left brain. Concentrate on pictures that come into your mind when you are reading, describe actions with words, memorize facts to music, and keep score in your head to strengthen the connection between your right and left brain (Healy 1987). These are actually left brain modes of thinking used to describe right brain concepts, and a right brain way of looking at things to understand materials organized in a left brain manner.

Although the suggestions for strengthening the connection between right and left brain thinking aren't specifically related to choreography, they do have applications in dance. When you are making a dance, you can focus on the essence of the inspiration and describe the inspiration with words. Writing an outline of your dance as you listen to the music can be helpful, as is going back and forth between visual images and verbal descriptions when you create a dance. You can also use both right and left brain modes of thinking during dance making by picturing various movements in your mind. Then, you can shift to the left brain mode to select or discard movements and arrange the movements in an order. Finally, you can return to the right brain to keep track of the form and development of your dance from beginning to end. I believe in using improvisation to discover movements for a dance. When you use improvisation, however, you work in the right brain mode because movements appear; as they appear you perform them with your body. In other words, there is no attempt to organize, evaluate, or discard any of the movements. Later, you use your left brain to organize or discard movements.

Create Structure: Connections for Reflection

1. Think about your inspiration again, and imagine how many parts you want to have in your dance.
2. Imagine the order of the parts of your dance.
3. Decide which movement sequences and their variations fit into each part of your dance.
4. Connect the movement sequences to create the different parts of your dance.
5. Have someone videotape you as you perform your dance.
6. Watch the video to determine whether your dance has a beginning, middle, and end.
7. Does the form of your dance suit the movement style?
8. Does the form of your dance fit your inspiration?
9. Does your dance resemble the dance you saw in your imagination?
10. Draw a diagram that describes the overall form of your dance.
11. Write a description of the overall form of your dance.

Step 7: Designing Your Dance

You already know one of the most basic rules of dance form—that a dance has a beginning, middle, and end. Dances should also have unity, continuity, and a sense of development through time. A well-formed dance also has enough variety to keep the audience interested, yet it has sufficient repetition so that the viewer can identify with some of the movements by seeing them again. It is helpful to follow such rules when you first learn to make dances, because such rules teach you about form in an established way. Once you understand form in the traditional sense, you can use this understanding to create dances that follow your unique sense of form.

I have discovered that some of the most innovative visual artists began painting in a realistic style, using a traditional sense of form. Recently, I studied the works of Mexican muralist Diego Rivera and found that Rivera's early works were realistic. Rivera also studied and painted in Europe, where he worked in the style of some of the modern painters such as Picasso. Later, Rivera returned to Mexico where he developed his distinctive style of painting based on native Mexican art. The point is that Rivera was able to develop his own style only after he had absorbed a traditional sense of form by painting realistically and by copying forms used by other artists. Picasso followed a similar path in this artistic development. Today, we identify Picasso with an abstract, cubist style of painting; but as a young man he also studied and created works with a more traditional sense of form.

Gestalt psychologists are also interested in the concept of the whole and how the parts of the whole fit together. These psychologists look at the whole, however, by examining how humans see their world at one point in time. In chapter 5 you explored the idea of pattern. Remember that you can create patterns and identify them in your surroundings. In the same sense, you create wholes from visual input and recognize them from input that comes to you. This spontaneous tendency to organize input into wholes is known as grouping input into *Gestalten*. Thus, *gestalt* is another word for whole. The principles of gestalt psychology can be used to describe how separate items in your visual field are attracted and create a whole. The following laws of visual perception apply: proximity, similarity, continuity, and closure (see figures 9.4, 9.5, and 9.6). Proximity means to be near. Thus, visual components that are closer

FIGURE 9.4　Group of dancers with similar body shapes standing in close proximity are seen as a whole.

FIGURE 9.5   The round objects are very close together and are seen as a curved line.

FIGURE 9.6   The dancer's arms are seen as a closed oval even though their fingers do not touch.

together are seen as a whole group. Visual components that are similar in shape, size, color, or movement quality are also seen as a whole. In terms of continuity, input that has the fewest interruptions is grouped together to form straight or curved lines in your visual field. Finally, closure refers to the fact that lines and shapes that are nearly closed or complete are seen as closed, because your eyes unconsciously close such lines (Zakia 1997).

Design Your Dance: Connections for Reflection

1. View the videotape of your dance again and decide whether it has a feeling of unity and continuity.
2. Do you think you have a balanced use of variety and repetition in your dance?
3. How many dancers do your want in your dance?
4. How can you distribute the movement sequences among your dancers?
5. How can you position or move your dancers to create relationships between them?
6. How do you want to group your dancers?
7. What types of visual lines do your want to create?
8. How do the groups and visual lines change as your dance progresses?

9. Teach the different parts of your dance to your dancers.

10. Experiment with different floor patterns, groupings, visual lines, and dancer-to-dancer relationships.

11. Videotape your dance again, but this time look at the relationships of your dancers as they move.

12. Do you think you have used the visual components proximity, similarity, continuity, and closure appropriately?

13. Do the relationships among your dancers fit the inspiration for your dance?

Step 8: Observing Your Dancers and Dance

A choreographer must be able to observe movement accurately during the rehearsal process and evaluate a dance as it nears completion. Good movement observation is based on learning to look at movement in a precise way, because the ability to observe movement is a skill in its own right. Skillful movement observation is dependent on several factors such as the focus (concentration) of the observer and the speed of the movements. The personal movement skill of the observer also affects the ability to observe. A good observer must study movement in several ways and have a visual strategy for looking at movement as well (Barrett 1979).

You can apply the general ideas for observation to your dance making by using the following suggestions. First, you must learn to concentrate on the components of the movements you use in creative work, such as pathway, energy, and body shape. Second, you may need to observe fast movements more than once. It may take you longer to choreograph and teach fast sections of your dance. Third, your personal movement skills are also important because a more skillful mover observes more accurately and has more movement possibilities to draw from while doing creative work. Finally, you need to look at dance movement from many viewpoints—something you have been doing throughout this book. For example, you have explored movement from the standpoint of body structure, the body parts that are moving, and the message. All of these viewpoints can, in turn, help you develop a movement observation strategy. The following are examples of different ways you can observe movement.

Joint action is easy to observe. Remember that some joints have a very limited movement potential, whereas other joints can be moved in more than one direction. Awareness of joint movement potential can help you be a more precise movement observer and give you more possible movements for use in dance making. Consider the actions bending and straightening. These two actions can be performed in many joints. You can also bend and straighten your whole body. In fact, you can create whole dances based on bending and straightening the joints of your body.

Next, you can observe which part of your body is moving and what type movement you are doing. You can move one arm or both arms as part of a dance sequence. You can also perform movement on the right or left side of your body, although it is possible to move both sides of your upper or lower body at the same time. You can move a part of your body or your whole body. You can also travel in space. To sample some of the creative possibilities, think about the number of body parts that you can use to perform a single nonlocomotor movement. Then, imagine how you can do one of the locomotor movements while performing nonlocomotor movements at the same time.

Observing joint action and body movement is a rather specific way to look at movement. In contrast, you can observe in a more general way—something you have already done in this book. First, you explored personal space and general space, then worked with directions, levels, and pathways in space. You worked with body supports, body shapes, movement speed, movement quality, and spatial relationships. Later, you built on these components by exploring body line, group shape, advanced pathways, transitions, order, and pattern. You followed this by using movement as a message, symbols, and different forms of imagery. You can use each of these components to observe movement. You can also see the creative potential in looking at movement in this way because you can combine the components in many different ways.

Observe Your Dancers: Connections for Reflection

1. You can observe movement in many different ways. What two methods of movement observation can you best use to improve the performance of your dance?

2. Use these two methods of observation when you watch the dancers perform your work.

3. Give suggestions and corrections to your dancers based on your observations.

4. Watch your dance again to determine whether your suggestions and corrections improved the performance. If your comments did not improve the performance, what other changes can you make in your dance?

Step 9: Preparing for Performance

When you prepare your dance for performance you need to think about many ideas. First, you must determine whether the movements in your dance are performed accurately in space. This means that if a movement is supposed to be done to the side, then the dancers must perform the movement straight to the side, not on a diagonal. Movement accuracy also refers to energy, timing, and body shape as well. So you need to make sure that the dancers perform all three of these elements in a way that matches your original conception of the dance. Accuracy is important because if you change the use of space, time, energy, or body shape in a dance, you also change the intent of your dance. For example, many times dancers think they are performing a movement in a certain way, but actually they are not. Some dancers think they are holding their arms out to the side in a slightly rounded position, but they are actually bending their arms at the elbow and wrist. In other words, dancers who perform a movement incorrectly do not have the right kinesthetic feeling of the movement or position.

You and your dancers must also focus while you practice your dance in preparation for performance. Relaxation is one of many techniques you can use to help improve focus. You can also improve focus by being positive. Deciding how a focused state feels is also important because when you are focused you are involved and one with the dance. Learning to focus takes practice, and you should use whatever works to help you and your dancers develop focusing abilities. The ability to focus should be part of a life plan. This means having enough rest, proper nutrition, quality relationships, and a balance of work and play. When focus wanders, you or your dancers need to learn to refocus quickly. Concentrate on words, ideas, or feelings connected with a focused state. For example, taking time to breathe deeply helps me relax and improves my concentration.

You can also prepare for a performance by using images during rehearsals. Remember that images can be visual or kinesthetic. Visual images describe how movements should look, and kinesthetic images give your dancers the body feeling they should experience in a movement. Choose your words carefully when you describe images, and make sure your inspiration is the model for each image you use. You and your dancers should avoid marking (a superficial performance of steps and gestures in a dance by using approximations instead of the full range of motion and expression) during rehearsals, because marking can become a habit that carries over into performance. Connecting with the appropriate visual and kinesthetic images can help dancers perform from the inside rather than mark or perform at a superficial level.

Another excellent way to prepare for a performance is to videotape your piece. I found that my dances improved immensely after a session with the video camera. As the choreographer you can make many suggestions to improve the performance of your dance. For some reason when performers see themselves in action, their performance improves more rapidly. Finally, performing your dance for a group of outsiders or small audience is helpful. There is nothing like performing in front of a live audience to energize dancers and get them to put forth their best effort.

Prepare for Performance: Connections for Reflection

1. Watch your dancers, making sure that they perform their movements accurately in terms of the movement elements and other important aspects of your dance. You can also see whether you perform your own movements accurately by watching yourself on videotape.

2. Create a positive atmosphere in your rehearsals.

3. Help your dancers develop a focused state of mind and body.

4. Think of visual and kinesthetic images that can help you and your dancers improve their performance of specific movements in your dance.

5. Videotape your dance again after using the previous suggestions. Then, watch the video to see whether performance has improved.

6. As you watch, point to places in your dance that have improved and where your dance still needs work.

Summary

You've gone through the steps, explored your own style, created your own movements, choreographed your own dance, and saw how it played out. As you continue in your dancing experience, go back to the concepts you learned in this book—from the basics of isolating movement to the creative expression based on an inspiration. Use these concepts to remind yourself of the millions of combinations possible in dance making and remember to constantly challenge yourself to do it again and again.

Challenges and Reflections

Select a new source for your inspiration. Do any mental pictures of objects from the real world or more abstract images come to mind? Explore possible movement responses and create movement phrases based on each image. Link the phrases together to create longer sequences of movement. Next, create variations of each sequence, and decide whether you want to repeat a sequence at any other point in the dance. Then, find an order for the sequences, and provide transitions that link them together. Next, arrange and design your dance for the performance space. This means deciding how your dancers will relate to each other in the stage space and how you group and regroup your dancers as the dance progresses.

- Perform your dance as you videotape it.
- Decide whether the movement phrases you created fit your inspiration. In other words, describe the similarities between your inspiration and the movements. Use the movement components such as the elements, body line, pathway, and pattern to make this comparison. Describe the dynamics in each phrase. Did any of the phrases begin with a burst of energy and end slowly, or did they begin slowly with sustained energy and pick up in speed and power by the end of the phrase?
- Describe the overall form of the dance you created. Be sure to include how the dance begins, what happens in the middle, and how it ends.
- Does your dance have unity and continuity?
- Are the transitions in your dance noticeable, or do they blend with the movements that come before and after them?
- Do you think you use repetition and variation appropriately in your dance? Explain why you answered yes or no to this question.
- Do you like the way you arrange and group your dancers in the performance space? Are these groupings appropriate for the inspiration for your dance?
- How can you improve the performance of your dance?
- Challenge yourself by creating other dances using the same nine steps.

Glossary

abstract—A type of dance that communicates no message or that communicates only the essence of the real thing.

abstraction—Process of removing, separating from, or condensing something to its essence.

accent—An emphasis, or stress, on specific musical beats or on particular movements.

accuracy—The ability to do a movement as demonstrated without changing the use of the elements.

adaptor—A form of body communication that uses movement in an unconscious way to release stress or deal with boredom.

affect display—A form of body communication that uses movement to convey emotions or feelings.

Alexander Technique—A body therapy system that deals with correcting misalignments in the body and other bad habits.

alignment—The placement of body segments so that the ear, shoulder, hip, knee, and ankle are as close as possible to a straight vertical line.

aliveness—Quality that contributes to movement dynamics and projection.

anatomical image—Mental picture of specific parts of the human body, which is used to inspire movement.

ankh—An ancient Egyptian symbol that represents life. It is shaped as a cross with a loop at the top.

anorexia nervosa—An eating disorder in which people refuse to eat normal amounts of food.

arabesque—A ballet pose in which the body is supported on one leg with the other leg extended to the back. The arms are held in various positions.

arabesque allongée—An extended, or stretched-out, form of the basic arabesque.

arc—A curved path in space.

arch—A pose in which the upper body is curved to the back.

asymmetrical—An unbalanced body shape or grouping of dancers.

attitude—A dance pose in which the weight is supported on one leg while the other leg is lifted with a bent knee.

axial—A movement in which the dancer remains in one spot. Also known as nonlocomotor movement.

axis—A point or center around which movement takes place. A long line around which the body can twist.

balance—To be in a state of equilibrium. One of the movement principles.

balance and compensation—Maintenance of equilibrium through counterbalance of weight of one part of the body with another.

balanced body—State in which muscles on opposite sides of the body are equal or nearly equal in elasticity and strength.

ball and socket joint—A place in the body where bones meet. Ball and socket joints can bend, straighten, move side to the side, and twist. The shoulder and hip are examples of such joints.

ballet—A dance form that uses traditional steps, positions, and body carriage. It originated before the 20th century. Also a dance or choreography.

Bartenieff Fundamentals—Body therapy system that emphasizes wholeness and integration of moving body parts.

beat—The basic, steady pulse in dance and music. Same as pulse.

bend—A nonlocomotor movement in which adjoining body segments move closer together.

biaxial joint—A place in the body where bones meet. Biaxial joints can bend, straighten, and move side to side.

body awareness—The act of being conscious of movements of the body, parts of the body, or of kinesthetic feelings in the body.

body feeling—How a position or movement feels in your body.

body image—A picture you have in your mind of your body.

body language—Placing the body in a particular way or using movements that send a message.

body memory—The skill of remembering the kinesthetic feelings of movements.

body perception—The act of tuning into feelings or sensations from the body.

body therapy—A system of theories and actions used to rid the body of bad or inefficient movements.

bound flow—A restricted use of energy in movement.

breathing—The act of inhaling and exhaling. Used to help movement come alive. One of the movement principles.

cardinal plane—The two-dimensional shapes or markers used to describe movement. There are three cardinal planes (horizontal, sagittal, and frontal) positioned at right angles to each other. Each passes through the center of the body.

center of gravity—The most dense part of the body, usually located slightly below the navel.

center point of balance—A point in the torso located where the two sides of the rib cage come together. Used to stabilize and balance the body.

centering—Process of locating both the physical and psychological centers of the body to achieve a feeling of being aligned and together. One of the movement principles.

chaîné turn—A series of fast, traveling turns that are connected.

character—A person in a play or dance that has qualities that cause him or her to stand out.

choreographer—One who discovers movement and organizes it into dances.

choreography—Many sequences of movement that add together to produce a whole dance with a beginning, middle, and end. Used interchangeably with the term *dance.*

classical ballet—Dance form that originated before the 20th century. The first ballets were choreographed and performed in the 17th century.

closure—The tendency to see familiar lines and shapes as complete or closed when they are actually incomplete.

collapse—A use of energy in which the dancer gives in to gravity.

condyloid joint—A place in the body where bones meet. Condyloid joints can bend, straighten, and move side to side.

conscious—The state of being aware or knowing what one is doing.

continuity—A principle of dance form that provides a natural and organized progression of movement so that one phrase flows or connects with the next.

contour—The outline or outside edge of a body shape or grouping of dancers.

contraction—A body position that forms the shape of the letter C. Shortening of fibers within a muscle.

corps—A ballet term for a group of dancers that perform together.

counterbalance—A position or movement in which one side of the body is used to offset the weight of the other side of the body.

creative process—Act of making or causing a work to come into existence.

cubism—A school of modern painting that pictures people and objects as cubes or other geometric shapes rather than as they actually appear.

curl—A nonlocomotor movement in which the opposite sides of the body are brought closer together as the body is lowered to the floor.

cutaneous receptors—Proprioceptors that relay information about pressure, temperature, or touch at the surface of the body.

dance making—The act of creating movements and shaping movements into a dance.

dance notation—Various shorthand systems for recording dance movements.

Delsarte System of Expression—A codified system of poses and gestures that communicate a feeling or message. Created by Francois Delsarte.

demi-plié—A dance movement in which the knees bend and straighten while the heels remain on the floor.

design—Lines, patterns, and shapes created with the body and with movement.

développé—A movement in ballet in which the gesturing foot is drawn up to the supporting knee and unfolded so that the foot moves away from the body.

diagram—An outline of the structure of a dance or part of a dance.

diaphragm—An anatomical structure separating the chest and abdominal cavities, which moves in the process of breathing.

direct image—Process of visualizing movement in your mind before performing it.

direction—One aspect of the movement element of space. In dance, the eight basic directions in which a dancer can move or face the body are forward, backward, right, left, and the four diagonals.

directed tensions—Lines and shapes in a dance or painting that have a sense of movement about them when experienced visually.

dynamic balance—Maintenance of equilibrium during movement.

dynamics—The loud and soft aspects of music. Can also refer to the use of energy and timing of movement.

eating behavior—Patterns of food intake.

ectomorph—A body type characterized by long, lean limbs and little body fat.

elasticity—Range of motion allowed at a joint. It is dependent on the degree of muscle tightness.

elements—A method of analyzing movement by looking at the use of space, time, energy, and body shape.

elevation—A movement that goes into the air.

emblem—A form of body communication that sends a message. Emblems have a meaning without being connected to words.

endomorph—A body type that is soft and rounded and usually has an excess of fatty tissue.

endurance—The ability to continue moving for an extended time.

energy—One of the elements of movement. Energy propels movement and causes changes in movement or body position. Used interchangeably with the word *force*.

equilibrium—A state of balance.

essence—The fundamental nature of an object or person.

exploration—A process producing spontaneous movement based on suggestions from a leader or from written instructions.

exploration framework—A method of initiating movement exploration by focusing on your response to an inspiration.

extension—A movement in which the space between two adjoining body segments widens.

fall and recovery—Doris Humphrey's theory that all dancing goes back and forth between two points: the vertical and the horizontal, or life and death.

fan kick—A movement in jazz dance in which the leg moves through a sweeping arc by crossing in front of the body and then up and out to the side.

feedback—The difference between an actual state in your body and your movement goal as a result of your kinesthetic sense. Also refers to a teacher's corrections after observing students perform movement.

Feldenkrais Method—Body therapy system that increases body awareness to correct movement problems.

felt-thought—The general body feeling that precedes the ability to verbalize a thought or idea.

Feuillet—A method of recording dances, which was created by Raoul Feuillet in the 18th century.

fifth position—A placement of the body in which both legs are turned out with the heel of the front foot next to the toe of the back foot.

figure-ground—The separation of the visual field into aspects that stand out and those that make up the background.

first position—A dance position in which the heels touch and both legs are turned out.

flexed foot—A position in which the ankle is bent rather than straight.

flexibility—Range of motion allowed at joint. Muscle tightness and structural differences limit flexibility.

flexion—A movement in which the space between two adjoining body segments narrows.

floor pattern—A pathway traced on the floor by using locomotor movements.

flow—A descriptor used by Rudolf Laban for describing use of energy in a movement.

focal point—A spot where attention is drawn onstage or in a painting.

focus—To concentrate on sensations or feelings arising from the body.

form—The overall shape, organization, and development of many phrases to constitute a whole dance.

free flow—The way in which a dancer uses energy; uncontrolled, carefree movements.

frontal plane—The two-dimensional shape that divides the front half of the body from the back half of the body.

gallop—A locomotor movement that travels forward with one foot chasing the other. Has the rhythm of step, together–step.

general space—An area in which a dancer travels by moving from one spot to another.

gestalt—Integrated structures and patterns making up a whole that cannot be derived from any single part.

Gestalt psychology—A school of psychology that looks at human responses to input as a whole rather than as separate parts.

gesture—A movement of the body or part of the body used to express or emphasize ideas or feelings.

glide—A locomotor movement that is performed smoothly while keeping the center at a constant level from the floor.

Golgi tendon organ—A proprioceptor that relays information about force or tension in a muscle.

grand plié—A dance movement in which the knees bend deeply, the heels lift and return to the floor. Grand plié goes lower and takes longer than demi–plié.

gravity—A natural force that draws all bodies toward the earth. One of the movement principles.

harmony—A series of simultaneous tones in music.

hinge joint—A place in the body where bones meet. Hinge joints can bend and straighten only.

hop—A locomotor movement that pushes off and lands on the same foot.

horizontal plane—A two-dimensional shape that is parallel to the floor and that cuts through the center of the body. Used interchangeably with *transverse plane.*

hyperextension—A movement in which adjoining segments of the body move apart, and the joint goes beyond a normal straight position.

icosahedron—A geometric form that intersects the three planes of movement and connects their corners. Designed by Rudolf Laban.

illustrator—A form of body communication that emphasizes a point. Illustrators must be connected to words to have a specific meaning.

image—A mental picture or kinesthetic feeling.

improvisation—A process producing spontaneous movements stemming from a specific inspiration. A more complete and inner-motivated spontaneous movement experience than exploration.

indirect image—A movement inspiration that comes from outside the body.

inner sensing—The awareness of feelings from the body.

inspiration—The starting point for movement exploration, improvisation, and dance making.

involvement—The state of having one's attention occupied. Movement experiences in which there is more than a superficial level of attention.

isolation—Dance movements restricted to one area or part of the body.

jazz dance—A dance form that developed with jazz music. Its appeal is through the use of energy, variety, and syncopation.

joint—A place in the body where bones meet. Joints vary in their potential for movement.

joint action—A movement produced by muscles and occurring at the point at which bones connect.

joint angle—Angle formed between two adjacent body segments.

joint receptors—A proprioceptor that relays information about exact joint position.

jump—A locomotor movement that takes off and lands on both feet.

kinesiologist—A person who studies the structure and movements of the body.

kinesphere—A term coined by Rudolf Laban to describe the reach space around the body.

kinesthesis—Relating to aspects of body sensations, position, movement, and tension.

kinesthetic awareness—The act of being conscious of the body, parts of the body, or feelings from the body. Used interchangeably with the term *body awareness.*

kinesthetic body—Second form of the body that is nonphysical. A representation of the body in the brain that develops from having an awareness of different parts of the body. Similar to body image.

kinesthetic feeling—The type of sensation a movement produces in the body.

kinesthetic image—A movement inspiration that describes the body feeling that accompanies an action.

kinesthetic perception—Awareness of information from the kinesthetic sense.

kinesthetic sensation—The process of receiving impressions and input through the body or kinesthetic sense.

kinesthetic sense—Human sense that monitors body position, movement, orientation, and tension.

kyphosis—Misalignment of the spine producing an enlarged backward curve in the upper back.

Labanotation—A system of dance notation created by Rudolf Laban. Written symbols are used to describe movement so that it can be reproduced accurately.

language—What the characters say onstage in a play. The language of a play depicts its action and meaning.

laterality—Applying to one side of the body.

leap—A locomotor movement in which the performer takes off from one foot and lands on the other foot as the body traces an arc through space.

left brain mode—Capacity of the human brain to analyze input in a step-by-step way, emphasizing linear, sequential thought.

legato—A manner of performing movement or music in a smooth, connected manner.

level—One of the aspects of the movement element space. The three basic levels are high, middle, and low.

line—A pathway that can be visually traced between two points on the body. Also the use of body parts to create lines.

line of gravity—An imaginary line that extends from the body's center of gravity to the ground.

literal—A dance that communicates a story or message.

locomotor movement—Movements that travel across space.

lordosis—A misalignment of the spine producing an increased forward curve in the neck or small of the back.

lumbar—Part of the spine that makes up the small of the back.

lunge—A dance movement in which the performer reaches one leg away from the body and takes the weight on that leg while bending the knee.

lyric—A term describing a movement style that is smooth, calm, and controlled.

marking—The use of approximate steps and gestures to help dancers memorize the sequence of movements in a combination. Dancers don't show the full range of motion or expression while marking a combination.

measure—A unit or grouping in music.

melody—A forward progression of consecutive tones.

mental picture—A visual image that you can see in your mind.

mental practice—Act of reviewing movements in the mind without actually performing them. Used interchangeably with *mental rehearsal.*

mental rehearsal—Act of reviewing movements in the mind without actually performing them. Used interchangeably with *mental practice.*

mesomorph—A body type characterized by large bones and thick muscles.

midrange—The midpoint of the distance a body part can be moved at a joint.

Mind Body Centering—Body therapy system that emphasizes movement work with the various body systems.

mind-body connection—The concept that the mind and body are not separate, but related.

mirror—To copy the movements of another while facing that person.

misalignment—Positioning of individual body segments in which some or all of them are out of line. Usually refers to placement in the spine.

modern dance—A performance dance form created at the beginning of the 20th century. Creative work is an important part of modern dance.

Motif Notation—Written symbols used to describe the general quality or essence of a movement, not the actual movements.

motion capture—Computer technology used to digitally map the movement of a dancing figure.

motivation—The beginning point for movement exploration or improvisation. Used interchangeably with term *inspiration.*

motor response—A reaction to input using movement.

movement descriptor—Words used to tell how a movement looks or feels in the body.

movement elements—A method of analyzing an action by looking at the use of space, time, energy, and body shape.

movement exploration—A process resulting in spontaneous movement beginning with an inspiration or motivation. An outer-motivated movement process.

movement potential—Movement possibilities found in various joints.

movement principle—A fundamental law of body movement or position.

movement range—The distance a body part can be moved at a joint.

multisensory—The process of stimulating more than one human sense.

muscle memory—The ability to re-create movements based on how they feel in the body.

muscle spindle—A proprioceptor that relays information about muscle contraction.

narrative—A dance that tells a story.

negative space—Empty space surrounded by parts of the body, or empty space between two or more dancers.

nonliteral choreography—A dance that emphasizes movement variation and design with no intent to tell a story.

nonlocomotor movement—An action in which a dancer remains in one spot.

nonverbal communication—Sending a message with the body. Communicating without words.

oblique—Having a slanted position in relation to the floor and walls of a room.

on point—The act of dancing on the tips of the toes while the foot is supported in a boxed slipper.

opposition—A pulling sensation between the upper and lower halves of the body, or between the right and left sides of the body. Used to balance body segments.

order—The organization or arrangement of actions in a particular movement sequence or in a dance.

organic—A dance or movement sequence that has an organization of parts similar to the organization of shapes and parts in nature.

orientation—The position of the body with respect to its surroundings.

pantomime—Realistic movements used for the purposes of expression.

parallel—A body position in which both feet are positioned so that the toes point straight ahead.

passé—A position in ballet in which the working leg is drawn up to the knee of the supporting leg.

pathway—Designs traced in the air as you move body parts or the whole body through space.

pattern—The organization of movements into relationships that can be identified by an observer.

perception—Conscious awareness of input through the use of the senses.

percussive—A use of energy that is powerful and explosive.

personal space—The area immediately surrounding your body and into which you can reach without changing location in space.

phrase—The smallest and simplest unit of a dance.

picture image—A mental picture that is realistic or resembles something real. Can be used to inspire movement.

pitch—The high and low aspects of music.

placement—The positioning of body parts one above the other so that they are close to a straight line.

plane—A flat, level surface; a two-dimensional shape.

plié—A dance movement in which the knees bend, then straighten.

plot—The plan of action in a book or play.

plumb bob—A weight on the end of a string, used to check body alignment.

podiascope—A device used to check the placement of weight on the feet.

pose—A stationary body position.

positive forms—The actual location of the body or of parts of the body.

posture—Placement of the body's segments one above the other. Also the body's response to situations.

progressive relaxation—A system designed to rid the body of tension by developing an awareness of its existence.

pronation—To roll inward on the arches of the feet.

proprioceptors—Set of sensory receptors that monitor body movement and position. They are located in muscles, tendons, joints, and the inner ear.

proximity—The tendency to see two or more visual elements as a group when the elements are positioned close together.

pull—A nonlocomotor movement in which you use one body part or the whole body to perform dragging or tugging actions.

pulse—The basic, steady beat in dance and music. Also known as *beat*.

push—A nonlocomotor movement in which the whole body or a body part presses against an imagined or real object.

quality—The way a dancer uses energy while doing a movement.

realistic—Presenting or picturing things as they appear in the natural world.

regulator—A form of body communication used to signal interest in interacting with another person.

relaxed alertness—A state of mind that is both focused and relaxed at the same time. Used interchangeably with *relaxed concentration*.

relaxed concentration—A state of mind that is both focused and relaxed at the same time. Used interchangeably with *relaxed alertness*.

relevé—A ballet movement in which the heels lift off the floor so that the weight is supported on the ball or balls of the feet.

repetition—A principle of choreographic form in which movements are repeated in a dance.

rhythm—A structure of patterned movement occurring through time.

rhythmic pattern—The organization of movements or sounds into recognizable groupings or relationships.

rib cage—The curved bones enclosing the chest cavity.

right brain mode—Capacity of the human brain to think in wholes, emphasizing patterns, relationships, and imagery.

rotation—Movements that twist around the long axis of a bone or around the length of the spine.

run—A locomotor movement in which both feet are off the ground for an instant. Faster than a walk.

sagittal plane—A two-dimensional shape that extends to the front and back from the middle of the body.

scales—Sequences of movement devised by Rudolf Laban. The sequence links points in space in a specific order.

second position—A placement of body parts in which the arms are held out to the side with the feet placed under the shoulders.

segment—Any of the parts, such as the head or forearm, into which the body is divided.

sensation—Impressions from input received through sensory organs.

sequence—A series of actions longer than a phrase but much shorter than a part of a dance. Similar to a *combination.*

shake—A nonlocomotor movement involving short, quick, repetitive actions.

shape—One of the elements of movement. Refers to an arrangement of body parts of one dancer or of a group of dancers.

sighting—The ability to see relationships between parts of a visual subject.

sign—Something that points the way to observers.

sink—A nonlocomotor movement in which the body goes slowly to the floor.

skip—A locomotor movement that goes into the air from one foot and lands on the same foot. A step–hop.

slide—A locomotor movement in which the feet are moved apart and drawn together as the body goes into the air.

solar plexus—The center point of balance. Duncan used this term in reference to expression.

space—One of the elements of movement. Direction, level, size, focus, and pathway are aspects of space.

spectacle—What is seen onstage. Can refer to actions onstage such as a swordfight or dance number or to props, costumes, or movements of the technical equipment.

speed—The rate at which movement occurs. Also its velocity.

staccato—An action or sound performed quickly with breaks in the movement or sound.

stage movement—Actions used by actors to go with their spoken words.

static balance—Maintenance of equilibrium in stationary positions.

stimulus—The beginning point for movement exploration or improvisation. Used interchangeably with *inspiration.*

straighten—A nonlocomotor movement in which adjoining body segments move apart.

strength—State of increased power from doing more work with the muscles.

structure—The way movements relate or are put together in a dance.

style—A characteristic manner of moving.

supinate—Rolling onto the outward edges of the feet.

suspended—Use of energy in which the movements appear to hover in midair.

sustained—Use of energy that is slow, smooth, and controlled.

sway—A nonlocomotor movement that involves taking the weight alternately from foot to foot so that the whole body goes from one side to the other.

swinging—Use of energy in which the body traces an arc in space. It is necessary to give in to gravity on the downward part of the arc and use energy during the upward action.

symbol—Something that stands for or represents something else.

symmetrical—Visually balanced body shape or grouping of dancers.

synesthesia—Experiences with one sense that produce imagined sensations in another sense.

tactile—Related to the sense of touch. Can be an inspiration for movement.

tai chi chuan—Chinese exercise system that uses interaction of hard and soft forces.

technique—Learning movement skills or movement coordination and control.

tempo—The speed of a movement.

tensegrity—The relationship between relaxation and tension.

tension and relaxation—One of the movement principles. Relates to the tightness and release of muscles.

texture—The density or sparseness of music. Also the quality of movement or the tactile aspects of a painting or sculpture.

theme—Message communicated in a dance. Also movements that fit together and are repeated and developed throughout a dance.

thoracic—Part of the spine making up the chest area.

tilt—A modern dance position or movement in which the body is off center. The body is supported on one leg, and the other leg is lifted high to the side.

timbre—The unique sound of different instruments or voices. Also known as *tone color*.

time—One of the elements of movement. Refers to the speed of an action.

tone color—The unique shadings of sound from various instruments and voices. Also known as *timbre*.

tone poem—Music created to follow expressive ideas and complement them.

tracer effect—The visual afterimage, or trail, left by a moving dancer or object.

transition—An aspect of choreographic form that provides a bridge between movements.

transverse plane—The two-dimensional shape that cuts through the center of the body. It is parallel to the floor. Used interchangeably with *horizontal plane*.

triaxial joint—A place in the body where bones meet. Triaxial joints can bend, straighten, move side to side, and twist.

turn—A nonlocomotor or locomotor movement in which the body changes position by rotating.

turnout—Positions in which the legs are rotated at the hip away from the middle of the body.

twist—A nonlocomotor movement in which the opposite ends of the body move in different directions or in which a body part turns around the long axis of a bone.

unconscious—The state of being unaware of your movements or the feeling of your movements.

underwater weighing—Method of determining the percentage of fat in the body by submerging the body in water.

uniaxial joint—A place in the body where bones meet. Uniaxial joints can bend and straighten only.

unity—A principle of choreographic form in which movements fit together in a way that forms a whole dance.

variation—The process of changing the elements of movement found in an action.

verbal cue—Words used by a teacher or leader to initiate and guide movements of others.

vertebra—One of the separate bones that make up the spine.

vestibular apparatus—A part of the kinesthetic sense that relays information about body position and movements of the head. Located in the inner ear.

vibratory—A use of energy that involves shaking or trembling.

virtual entity—The illusion an audience sees. It is different from the actual movements in a dance.

visual image—An inspiration for movement. Also a picture in the mind.

visual strategy—A plan or method for observing movement.

visual tension—An illusion or sense of movement created when you look at a dance or painting.

visualize—The process of forming a mental picture of an object or activity in the mind.

vocabulary of steps—The movements learned in a particular dance form.

volume—The fullnesss or loudness of a sound.

walk—A locomotor movement in which one foot is always on the ground.

weight—A movement descriptor used to describe the firmness or lightness of a movement. First used by Rudolf Laban.

whole—Fitting together or being complete. Having all the necessary elements or parts.

Bibliography

Arnheim, R. 1974. *Art and visual perception: A psychology of the creative eye*. Berkeley: University of California.

Asante, K.W., ed. 1996. *African dance: An artistic, historical and philosophical inquiry*. Trenton, NJ: Africa World Press.

Bardsley, K. 1992. Re-animations of Duncan master works: A four year project 1976-1980. In *Proceedings dance re-constructed: Modern dance art past, present, and future: 25th year retrospective Nikolais/Louis*. Rutgers State University of New Jersey Department of Dance.

Barrett, K.R. 1979. Observation of movement for teachers: Synthesis and implications. *Motor Skills: Theory Into Practice* 3: 67-76.

Becks-Malorny, U. 1994. *Wassily Kandinsky: The journey to abstraction*. Köln, Germany: Taschen.

Blair, F. 1986. *Isadora: Portrait of the artist as a woman*. New York: McGraw-Hill.

Blair, S. 2002a. Centering. [on line]. Available at http://www.swingworld.com/articles.

Blair, S. 2002b. 3-Toe Base. [on line]. Available at http://www.swingworld.com/articles.

Caine, R.N., and G. Caine. 1997. *Education on the edge of possibility*. Alexandria, VA: Association for Supervision and Curriculum Development.

Delsarte, F. 1887. *Delsarte system of oratory*. New York: Werner.

DeSpain, K. 2000. Digital dance: The computer artistry of Paul Kaiser. *Dance Research Journal* 32 (1): 18-23.

Edwards, B. 1999. *The new drawing on the right side of the brain*. New York: Tarcher/ Putnam.

Fast, J. 1994. *Body language in the workplace*. New York: Penguin.

Fitt, S.S. 1996. *Dance kinesiology*. New York: Schirmer Books.

Fontana, D. 1993. *The secret language of symbols*. San Francisco: Chronicle Books.

Forsythe, W., and R. Sulcas. 2000. *Improvisation technologies*. CD-ROM. Hatje Cantz Publishers.

Franklin, E. 1996. *Dance imagery for technique and practice*. Champaign, IL: Human Kinetics.

Garofola, L., ed. 1999. *José Limón: An unfinished memoir*. Middletown, CT: Wesleyan University.

Gardner, H. 1994. *The arts and human development*. New York: Basic Books.

Griffin-Pierce, T. 1992. *Earth is my mother, sky is my father*. Albuquerque: University of New Mexico.

Hackney, P. 1996. Making connections through Bartenieff fundamentals. In *Dance Kinesiology.* New York: Schirmer Books.

Hartley, L. 1995. *Wisdom of the body moving.* Berkeley, CA: North Atlantic Books.

Hatcher, J. 1996. *The art and craft of play writing.* Cincinnati: Story Press.

Hawkins, A.M. 1988. *Creating through dance.* Revised ed. Princeton, NJ: Princeton Books.

Hawkins, A.M. 1991. *Moving from within: A new method for dance making.* Pennington, NJ: A Cappella Books.

Healy, J.M. 1987. *Your child's growing mind: A guide to learning and brain development from birth to adolescence.* New York: Doubleday.

Houston, J. 1997. *The possible human.* Revised ed. New York: Tarcher/Putnam.

Howe, T., and J. Oldham. 1998. Posture and balance. In *Human Movement: An Introductory Text.* 4th ed. Edinburgh: Churchill Livingstone.

Humphrey, D. 1987. *The art of making dances.* 2nd ed. Princeton, NJ: Princeton Books.

Hutchinson, A.G. 1995. *Your move: A new approach to the study of movement and dance.* London: Gordon and Breach.

Jowitt, D. 1988. *Time and the dancing image.* Berkeley, CA: University of California.

Jung, C.G. 1964. *Man and his symbols.* New York: Anchor/Doubleday.

Knaster, M. 1996. *Discovering the body's wisdom.* New York: Bantam Books.

Langer, S.K. 1957. *Problems of art.* New York: Scribner's Sons.

Lessinger, C. 1996. The nature of the Feldenkrais method and its value to dancers. In *Dance Kinesiology.* New York: Schirmer Books.

Lidell, L. 1987. *The sensual body: The ultimate guide to body awareness and self-fulfillment.* New York: Simon and Schuster.

Maletic, V. 1987. *Body, space, expression: The development of Rudolf Laban's movement and dance concepts.* Berlin: Mouton de Gruyter.

Mazo, J.H. 2000. *Prime movers: The makers of modern dance in America.* 2nd ed. Hightstown, NJ: Princeton Books.

McDonagh, D. 1990. *The rise and fall and rise of modern dance.* Princeton, NJ: A Cappella Books.

McVickar Edwards, C.E. 1995. *Sunstories: Tales from around the world to illuminate the days and nights of our lives.* San Francisco: HarperSanFrancisco.

Minot, S. 1998. *The genres: The writing of poetry, fiction and drama.* 6th ed. Upper Saddle River, NJ: Prentice Hall.

Morris, D. 1994. *Body talk: The meaning of human gestures.* New York: Crown.

Orlick, T. 1998. *Embracing your potential.* Champaign, IL: Human Kinetics.

Overby, L.Y. 1990. The use of imagery by dance teachers—development and implementation of two research instruments. *Journal of Physical Education, Recreation and Dance* 61 (2): 24-27.

Overby, L.Y. 1992. A comparison of novice and experienced dancers' body awareness. *Dance: Current Selected Research* 3: 57-72.

Penrod, J., and J.G. Plastino. 1998. *The dancer prepares: Modern dance for beginners.* 4th ed. Mountain View, CA: Mayfield.

Plastino, J.G. 1990. Physical screening of the dancer: General methodologies and procedures. In *Preventing dance injuries: An interdisciplinary perspective.* Reston, VA: AAHPERD.

Pruzinsky, T., and T.F. Cash. 1990. Integrative themes in body-image development, deviance and change. In *Body Images: Development, Deviance, and Change.* New York: Guilford.

Richmond, V.P., and J.C. McCroskey. 2000. *Nonverbal behavior in interpersonal relations.* 4th ed. Boston: Allyn and Bacon.

Root-Berstein, R., and M. Root-Berstein. 1999. *Sparks of genius: The 13 thinking tools of the world's most creative people.* Boston: Houghton Mifflin.

Rugg, H. 1963. *Imagination.* New York: Harper and Row.

Schiffman, H.R. 1996. *Sensation and perception: An integrated approach.* 4th ed. New York: Wiley and Sons.

Scott, M. 1996. Laban movement analysis and Bartenieff fundamentals. In *Dance Kinesiology.* New York: Schirmer Books.

Shawn, T. 1954. *Every little movement: A book about Francois Delsarte.* Pennington, NJ: Dance Horizons/Princeton Books.

Siegel, M.B. 2001. The harsh and splendid heroines of Martha Graham. In *Moving History/Dancing Cultures.* Middletown, CT: Wesleyan University.

Simons, J. 2000. Reading the signs. *Rocky Mountain News,* 10 January.

Stodell, E. 1978. *The dance technique of Doris Humphrey and its creative potential.* Princeton, NJ: Princeton.

Stodell, E. 1984. *Deep song: The dance story of Martha Graham.* New York: Schirmer Books.

Sweigard, L.E. 1974. *Human movement potential: Its ideokinetic facilitation.* New York: Dodd, Mead.

Taylor, J., and C. Taylor. 1995. *Psychology of dance.* Champaign, IL: Human Kinetics.

Teck, K. 1994. *Ear training for the body: A dancer's guide to music.* Pennington, NJ: Princeton Books.

Turocy, C. 2001. Beyond *la danse noble:* Convention in choreography and dance performance at the time of Rameau's *Hippolyte et Aricie.* In *Moving History/Dancing Cultures.* Middletown, CT: Wesleyan University.

Zakia, R.D. 1997. *Perception and imaging.* Boston: Focal Press.

Zorn, J. 1968. *The essential Delsarte.* Metuchen, NJ: Scarecrow.

Index

Note: The italicized *f* and *t* following page numbers refer to figures and tables, respectively.

About the Author

Sandra Cerny Minton, PhD, was the coordinator of the dance program at the University of Northern Colorado at Greeley. She has taught and choreographed dance for more than 30 years and directed numerous concerts.

As an active member of the Colorado Dance Alliance; the National Dance Association of the American Alliance for Health, Physical Education, Recreation and Dance; and the National Dance Education Organization, Minton is well respected as a dance educator. She was a 2001 Fulbright Scholar and honored as the National Dance Association Scholar/Artist in 1999.

Sandra Minton earned her master's degree in dance education from the University of California at Los Angeles and earned her PhD in dance and related arts from the Texas Woman's University. The author of numerous articles and books on dance, she resides in Thornton, Colorado.

*You'll find
other outstanding
dance resources at*

www.HumanKinetics.com

In the U.S. call

800-747-4457

Australia 08 8277 1555
Canada 800-465-7301
Europe .... +44 (0) 113 255 5665
New Zealand 09-523-3462

HUMAN KINETICS
The Premier Publisher in Sports and Fitness
P.O. Box 5076 • Champaign, IL 61825-5076 USA